On the *Revival of the Religious Sciences* (*Iḥyāʾ ʿulūm al-dīn*)

"The *Iḥyāʾ ʿulūm al-dīn* is the most valuable and most beautiful of books."

—Ibn Khallikān (d. 681/1282)

"The *Iḥyāʾ ʿulūm al-dīn* is one of al-Ghazālī's best works."

—Aḥmad b. ʿAbd al-Ḥalīm (d. 728/1328)

"Any seeker of [felicity of] the hereafter cannot do without the *Iḥyāʾ ʿulūm al-dīn*"

—Tāj al-Dīn al-Subkī (d. 771/1370)

"The *Iḥyāʾ ʿulūm al-dīn* is a marvelous book containing a wide variety of Islamic sciences intermixed with many subtle accounts of Sufism and matters of the heart."

—Ibn Kathīr (d.774/1373)

"The *Iḥyāʾ ʿulūm al-dīn* is one of best and greatest books on admonition, it was said concerning it, 'if all the books of Islam were lost except for the *Iḥyāʾ* it would suffice what was lost.'"

—Ḥājjī Khalīfa Kātib Čelebī (d. 1067/1657)

"The *Iḥyāʾ* [*ʿulūm al-dīn*] is one of [Imām al-Ghazālī's] most noble works, his most famous work, and by far his greatest work'"

—Muḥammad Murtaḍā l-Zabīdī (d. 1205/1791)

On Imām al-Ghazālī

"Al-Ghazālī is [like] a deep ocean [of knowledge]."

—Imām al-Ḥaramayn al-Juwaynī (d. 478/1085)

"Al-Ghazālī is the second [Imām] Shāfiʿī."

—Muḥammad b. Yaḥyā l-Janzī (d. 549/1154)

"Abū Ḥāmid al-Ghazālī, the Proof of Islam (Ḥujjat al-Islām) and the Muslims, the Imām of the imāms of religion, [is a man] whose like eyes have not seen in eloquence and elucidation, and speech and thought, and acumen and natural ability."

—ʿAbd al-Ghāfir b. Ismāʿīl al-Fārisī (d. 529/1134)

"[He was] the Proof of Islam and Muslims, Imām of the imāms of religious sciences, one of vast knowledge, the wonder of the ages, the author of many works, and [a man] of extreme intelligence and the best of the sincere."

—Imām al-Dhahabī (d. 748/1347)

"Al-Ghazālī is without doubt the most remarkable figure in all Islam."

—T.J. DeBoer

". . . A man who stands on a level with Augustine and Luther in religious insight and intellectual vigor."

—H.A.R. Gibb

"I have to some extent found, and I believe others can find, in the words and example of al-Ghazālī a true *iḥyāʾ* . . ."

—Richard J. McCarthy, S.J.

The Forty Books of the Revival of the Religious Sciences (*Iḥyāʾ ʿulūm al-dīn*)

The Quarter of Worship

1 The Book of Knowledge
2 The Principles of the Creed
3 The Mysteries of Purification
4 The Mysteries of the Prayer
5 The Mysteries of Charity
6 The Mysteries of Fasting
7 The Mysteries of the Pilgrimage
8 The Etiquette of the Recitation of the Qurʾān
9 Invocations and Supplications
10 The Arrangement of the Litanies and the Exposition of the Night Vigil

The Quarter of Customs

11 The Proprieties of Eating
12 The Proprieties of Marriage
13 The Proprieties of Acquisition and Earning a Living
14 The Lawful and the Unlawful
15 The Proprieties of Friendship and Brotherhood
16 The Proprieties of Retreat
17 The Proprieties of Travel
18 The Proprieties of the Audition and Ecstasy
19 The Commanding of Right and the Forbidding of Wrong
20 The Proprieties of Living and the Prophetic Mannerisms

The Quarter of Perils

21 The Exposition of the Wonders of the Heart
22 Training the Soul, Refining the Character, and Treating the Ailments of the Heart
23 Overcoming the Two Desires
24 The Bane of the Tongue
25 The Censure of Anger, Malice, and Envy
26 The Censure of This World
27 The Censure of Greed and the Love of Wealth
28 The Censure of Fame and Hypocritical Ostentation
29 The Censure of Pride and Vanity
30 The Censure of Deceit

The Quarter of Deliverance

31 On Repentance
32 On Patience and Thankfulness
33 On Fear and Hope
34 On Poverty and Abstinence
35 On Unity and Trust
36 On Love, Longing, Intimacy, and Contentment
37 On Intention, Sincerity, and Truthfulness
38 On Vigilance and Accounting
39 On Contemplation
40 On the Remembrance of Death and the Hereafter

بِسۡمِ ٱللَّهِ ٱلرَّحۡمَٰنِ ٱلرَّحِيمِ

THE MYSTERIES OF PURIFICATION

Kitāb asrār al-ṭahāra

Book 3 of

The Revival of the Religious Sciences

Iḥyāʾ ʿulūm al-dīn

AL-GHAZĀLĪ

Kitāb asrār al-ṭahāra

THE MYSTERIES OF PURIFICATION

BOOK 3 of the *Iḥyāʾ ʿulūm al-dīn*

THE REVIVAL OF THE RELIGIOUS SCIENCES

TRANSLATED *from the* ARABIC *with an* INTRODUCTION *and* NOTES *by* M. FOUAD ARESMOUK *and* M. ABDURRAHMAN FITZGERALD

FONS VITAE
2017

The Mysteries of Purification, Book 3 of
The Revival of the Religious Sciences first published in 2017 by

Fons Vitae
49 Mockingbird Valley Drive
Louisville, KY 40207 USA

www.fonsvitae.com

The Fons Vitae Ghazali Series
Library of Congress Control Number: 2017931453
ISBN 978-1-94-1610-31-2

Copyediting and indexing: Valerie Joy Turner
Book design and typesetting: www.scholarlytype.com
Text typeface: Adobe Minion Pro 11/13.5

Cover art courtesy of National Library of Egypt, Cairo.
Qurʾānic frontispiece to part 19. Written and illuminated by ʿAbdallāh b.
Muḥammad al-Ḥamadānī for Sultan Uljaytu 713/1313. Hamadan.

Printed in Canada

Contents

Editor's Note

This is the complete translation of the *Kitāb asrār al-ṭahāra*, *The Mysteries of Purification*, book 3 of the *Iḥyāʾ ʿulūm al-dīn* of Ḥujjat al-Islām, Abū Ḥāmid al-Ghazālī. It was translated from the published Arabic text by Dār al-Minhāj of Jedda (2011), which utilized additional manuscripts and early printed editions.

Arabic terms that appear in italics follow the transliteration system of the *International Journal of Middle East Studies*. Common era (CE) dates have been added. The blessings on prophets and others, as used by Imām al-Ghazālī, are represented in the original Arabic, as listed below.

Arabic	**English**	**Usage**
عَزَّوَجَلَّ	Mighty and majestic is He	On mention of God
سُبْحَانَهُۥوَتَعَالَىٰ	Exalted and most high is He	Used together or separately
صَلَّىٱللَّهُعَلَيْهِوَسَلَّمَ	Blessings and peace of God be upon him	On mention of the Prophet Muḥammad
عَلَيْهِٱلسَّلَامُ	Peace be upon him	On mention of one
عَلَيْهِمُٱلسَّلَامُ	Peace be upon them	or more prophets
رَضِيَٱللَّهُعَنْهُ	God be pleased with him	On mention of one or more
رَضِيَٱللَّهُعَنْهُمْ	God be pleased with them	Companions of the Prophet
رَضِيَٱللَّهُعَنْهَا	God be pleased with her	On mention of a female Companion of the Prophet
رَحِمَهُٱللَّهُ	God have mercy on him	On mention of someone who is deceased

The translators have included some of the footnotes and references provided by the editors of the Dār al-Minhāj edition. These footnotes include comments from Murtaḍā l-Zabīdī's *Itḥāf* (a detailed commentary on the *Iḥyāʾ ʿulūm al-dīn*) and identify many of Imām al-Ghazālī's sources. The translators provided explanatory footnotes where necessary; clarification in the text appears in hard brackets.

In addition, the editors have compiled a short biography of Imām al-Ghazālī with a chronology of important events in his life. This is followed by an extract from Imām al-Ghazālī's introduction to the *Iḥyāʾ ʿulūm al-dīn*; the editors hope this may serve as a guide to the *Revival of the Religious Sciences* for those reading Imām al-Ghazālī for the first time.

Biography of Imām al-Ghazālī

He is Abū Ḥāmid Muḥammad b. Muḥammad b. Muḥammad b. Aḥmad al-Ghazālī al-Ṭūsī; he was born in 450/1058 in the village of Ṭābarān near Ṭūs (in northeast Iran) and he died there, at the age of fifty-five, in 505/1111. Muḥammad's father died when he and his younger brother Aḥmad were still young; their father left a little money for their education in the care of a Sufi friend of limited means. When the money ran out, their caretaker suggested that they enroll in a *madrasa*. The *madrasa* system meant they had a stipend, room, and board. Al-Ghazālī studied *fiqh* in his hometown under a Sufi named Aḥmad al-Rādhakānī; he then traveled to Jurjān and studied under Ismāʿīl b. Masʿada al-Ismāʿīlī (d. 477/1084).

On his journey home his caravan was overtaken by highway robbers who took all of their possessions. Al-Ghazālī went to the leader of the bandits and demanded his notebooks. The leader asked, what are these notebooks? Al-Ghazālī answered: "This is the knowledge that I traveled far to acquire," the leader acquiesced to al-Ghazālī's demands after stating: "If you claim that it is knowledge that you have, how can we take it away from you?" This incident left a lasting impression on the young scholar. Thereafter, he returned to Ṭūs for three years, where he committed to memory all that he had learned thus far.

In 469/1077 he traveled to Nīshāpūr to study with the leading scholar of his time, Imām al-Ḥaramayn al-Juwaynī (d. 478/1085), at the Niẓāmiyya College; al-Ghazālī remained his student for approximately eight years, until al Juwaynī died. Al-Ghazālī was one of his most illustrious students, and al-Juwaynī referred to him as "a deep ocean [of knowledge]." As one of al-Juwaynī star pupils, al-Ghazālī used to fill in as a substitute lecturer in his teacher's absence. He also tutored his fellow students in the subjects that al-Juwaynī taught at the Niẓāmiyya. Al-Ghazālī wrote his first book, on the founding principles of legal theory (*uṣūl al-fiqh*), while studying with al-Juwaynī.

Very little is known about al-Ghazālī's family, though some biographers mention that he married while in Nīshāpūr; others note that he had married in Ṭūs prior to leaving for Nīshāpūr. Some accounts state that he had five children, a son who died early and four daughters. Accounts also indicate that his mother lived to see her son rise to fame and fortune.

After the death of al-Juwaynī, al-Ghazālī went to the camp (*al-muʿaskar*) of the Saljūq *wazīr* Niẓām al-Mulk (d. 485/1192). He stayed at the camp, which was a gathering place for scholars, and quickly distinguished himself among their illustrious company. Niẓām al-Mulk recognized al-Ghazālī's genius and appointed him professor at the famed Niẓāmiyya College of Baghdad.

Al-Ghazālī left for Baghdad in 484/1091 and stayed there four years—it was a very exciting time to be in the heart of the Islamic empire. At the Niẓāmiyya College he had many students, by some estimates as many as three hundred. In terms of his scholarly output, this was also a prolific period in which he wrote *Maqāṣid al-falāsifa, Tahāfut al-falāsifa, al-Mustaẓhirī,* and other works.

Al-Ghazālī was well-connected politically and socially; we have evidence that he settled disputes related to the legitimacy of the rule of the ʿAbbāsid caliph, al-Mustaẓhir (r. 487–512/1094–1118) who assumed his role as the caliph when he was just fifteen years old, after the death of his father al-Muqtadī (d. 487/1094). Al-Ghazālī issued a *fatwā* of approval of the appointment of al-Mustaẓhir and was present at the oath-taking ceremony.

In Baghdad, al-Ghazālī underwent a spiritual crisis, during which he was overcome by fear of the punishment of the hellfire. He became convinced that he was destined for the hellfire if he did not change his ways; he feared that he had become too engrossed in worldly affairs, to the detriment of his spiritual being. He began to question his true intentions: was he writing and teaching to serve God, or because he enjoyed the fame and fortune that resulted from his lectures. He experienced much suffering, both inward and outward; one day as he stood before his students to present a lecture, he found himself unable to speak. The physicians were unable to diagnose any physical malady. Al-Ghazālī remained in Baghdad for a time, then left his teaching post for the pilgrimage. He left behind fortune, fame, and influence. He was beloved by his numerous students and had many admirers, including the sultan; he was also envied by many. The presumption is that he left in the manner he did—ostensibly to undertake the pilgrimage—because if he had made public his intentions to leave permanently, those around him would have tried to convince him to remain and the temptation might have been too strong to resist.

After leaving Baghdad, he changed direction and headed toward Damascus; according to his autobiography he disappeared from the intellectual scene for ten years. This does not mean that he did not teach, but that he did not want to return to public life and be paid for teaching. This ten-year period can be divided into two phases. First, he spent two years in the East—in greater Syria and on the pilgrimage. We have evidence that while on his return to Ṭūs he appeared at a Sufi lodge opposite the Niẓāmiyya College in Baghdad. He spent the second phase of the ten-year period (the remaining eight years) in Ṭūs, where he wrote the famed *Iḥyāʾ ʿulūm al-dīn*, a work that was inspired by the change in his outlook that resulted from his spiritual crisis.

When he arrived back in his hometown in 490/1097, he established a school and a Sufi lodge, in order to continue teaching and learning. In 499/1106, Niẓām al-Mulk's son, Fakhr al-Mulk, requested that al-Ghazālī accept a teaching position at his old school, the Niẓāmiyya of Nīshāpūr. He accepted and taught for a time, but left this position in 500/1106 after Fakhr al-Mulk was assassinated by Ismāʿīlīs. He then returned to Ṭūs and divided his time between teaching and worship. He died in 505/1111 and was buried in a cemetery near the citadel of Ṭābarān.

Legacy and Contributions of al-Ghazālī

Al-Ghazālī's two hundred and seventy-three works span many disciplines and can be grouped under the following headings:

1. Jurisprudence and legal theory. Al-Ghazālī made foundational contributions to Shāfiʿī jurisprudence; his book *al-Wajīz* is major handbook that has been used in teaching institutions around the world; many commentaries have been written on it, most notably by Abū l-Qāsim ʿAbd al-Karīm al-Rāfiʿī (d. 623/1226). In legal theory, *al-Mustaṣfa min ʿilm al-uṣūl* is considered one of five foundational texts in the discipline.
2. Logic and philosophy. Al-Ghazālī introduced logic in Islamic terms that jurists could understand and utilize. His works on philosophy include the *Tahāfut al-falāsifa*, which has been studied far beyond the Muslim world and has been the subject of numerous commentaries, discussions, and refutations.
3. Theology, including works on heresiography in refutation of Bāṭinī doctrines. He also expounded on the theory of occasionalism.
4. Ethics and educational theory. The *Mīzān al-ʿamal* and other works such as the *Iḥyāʾ ʿulūm al-dīn* mention a great deal on education.
5. Spirituality and Sufism. His magnum opus, the *Iḥyāʾ ʿulūm al-dīn* is a pioneering work in the field of spirituality, in terms of its organization and its comprehensive scope.
6. Various fields. Al-Ghazālī also wrote shorter works in a variety of disciplines, including his autobiography (*al-Munqidh min al-ḍalāl*), works on Qurʾānic studies (*Jawāhir al-Qurʾān*), and political statecraft (*Naṣiḥat al-mūluk*).

Chronology of al-Ghazālī's Life

450/1058	Birth of al-Ghazālī at Ṭūs
c. 461/1069	Began studies at Ṭūs
c. 465/1073	Traveled to Jurjān to study
466–469/1074–1077	Studied at Ṭūs
469/1077	Studied with al-Jūwaynī at the Niẓāmiyya college in Nīshāpūr
473/1080	al-Ghazālī composed his first book, *al-Mankhūl fī l-uṣūl*
477/1084	Death of al-Fāramdhī, one of al-Ghazālī's teachers
25 Rabīʿ II 478/ 20 August 1085	Death of al-Jūwaynī; al-Ghazālī left Nīshāpūr
Jumāda I 484/ July 1091	Appointed to teach at the Niẓāmiyya college in Baghdad
10 Ramaḍān 485/ 14 October 1092	Niẓām-al-Mulk was assassinated
484–487/1091–1094	Studied philosophy
Muḥarrām 487/ February 1094	Attended the oath-taking of the new caliph, al-Mustaẓhir
487/1094	Finished *Maqāṣid al-falāsifa*
5 Muḥarrām 488/ 21 January 1095	Finished *Tahāfut al-falāsifa*
Rajab 488/ July 1095	Experienced a spiritual crisis
Dhū l-Qaʿda 488/ November 1095	Left Baghdad for Damascus
Dhū l-Qaʿda 489/ November – December 1096	Made pilgrimage and worked on the *Iḥyāʾ ʿulūm al-dīn*
Jumāda II 490/ May 1097	Taught from the *Iḥyāʾ ʿulūm al-dīn* during a brief stop in Baghdad
Rajab 490/June 1097	Seen in Baghdad by Abū Bakr b. al-ʿArabī
Fall 490/1097	Returned to Ṭūs

Dhū l-Ḥijja 490/ November 1097	Established a *madrasa* and a *khānqāh* in Ṭūs
Dhū l-Qaʿda 499/ July 1106	Taught at the Niẓāmiyya college in Nīshāpūr
500/1106	Wrote *al-Munqidh min al-ḍalāl*
500/1106	Returned to Ṭūs
28 Dhū l-Ḥijja 502/ 5 August 1109	Finished *al-Mustaṣfā min ʿilm al-uṣūl*
Jumada I 505/ December 1111	Finished *Iljām al-ʿawām ʿan ʿilm al-kalām*
14 Jumada II 505/ 18 December 1111	Imām al-Ghazālī died in Ṭūs

Eulogies in Verse

Because of him the lame walked briskly,
And the songless through him burst into melody.

On the death of Imām al-Ghazālī, Abū l-Muẓaffar Muḥammad al-Abiwardī said of his loss:

He is gone! and the greatest loss which ever afflicted me,
was that of a man who left no one like him among mankind.

About the *Revival of the Religious Sciences*

THE present work is book 3 of Imām al-Ghazālī's forty-volume masterpiece. Below is an excerpt from al-Ghazālī's introduction that explains the arrangement and purpose of the *Iḥyāʾ ʿulūm al-dīn*.

People have composed books concerning some of these ideas, but this book [the *Iḥyāʾ*] differs from them in five ways, by

1. clarifying what they have obscured and elucidating what they have treated casually;
2. arranging what they scattered and putting in order what they separated;
3. abbreviating what they made lengthy and proving what they reported;
4. omitting what they have repeated; and
5. establishing the truth of certain obscure matters that are difficult to understand and which have not been presented in books at all.

For although all the scholars follow one course, there is no reason one should not proceed independently and bring to light something unknown, paying special attention to something his colleagues have forgotten. Or they are not heedless about calling attention to it, but they neglect to mention it in books. Or they do not overlook it, but something prevents them from exposing it [and making it clear].

So these are the special properties of this book, besides its inclusion of all these various kinds of knowledge.

Two things induced me to arrange this book in four parts. The first and fundamental motive is that this arrangement in establishing what is true and in making it understandable is, as it were, inevitable because the branch of knowledge by which one approaches the hereafter is divided into the knowledge of [proper] conduct and the knowledge of [spiritual] unveiling.

By the knowledge of [spiritual] unveiling I mean knowledge and only knowledge. By the science of [proper] conduct I mean knowledge as well as action in accordance with that knowledge. This work will deal only with the science of [proper] conduct, and not with [spiritual] unveiling, which one is not permitted to record in writing, although it is the ultimate aim of saints and the ultimate aim of the sincere. The science of [proper] conduct is merely a path that leads to unveiling and only through that path did the prophets of God communicate with the people and lead them to Him. Concerning [spiritual] unveiling, the prophets عَلَيۡهِمُ ٱلسَّلَامُ spoke only figuratively and briefly through signs and symbols, because they realized the inability of people's minds to comprehend. Therefore since the scholars are heirs of the prophets, they cannot but follow in their footsteps and emulate their way.

The knowledge of [proper] conduct is divided into (1) outward knowledge, by which I mean knowledge of the senses and (2) inward knowledge, by which I mean knowledge of the functions of the heart.

The physical members either perform acts of prescribed worship, or acts that are in accordance with custom, while the heart, because it is removed from the senses and belongs to the world of dominion, is subject to either praiseworthy or blameworthy [influences]. Therefore it is necessary to divide this branch of knowledge into two parts: outward and inward. The outward part, which is connected to the senses, is subdivided into acts of worship and acts that pertain to custom. The inward part, which is connected to the states of the heart and the characteristics of the soul, is subdivided into blameworthy states and praiseworthy states. So the total makes four divisions of the sciences of the practice of religion.

The second motive [for this division] is that I have noticed the sincere interest of students in jurisprudence, which has become popular among those who do not fear God ﷻ but who seek to boast and exploit its influence and prestige in arguments. It [jurisprudence] is also divided into four quarters, and he who follows the style of one who is beloved becomes beloved.

بِسْمِ ٱللَّهِ ٱلرَّحْمَٰنِ ٱلرَّحِيمِ

وَالصَّلَاةُ وَالسَّلَامُ عَلَى رَسُولِهِ الْكَرِيمِ وَعَلَى آلِهِ وَأَصْحَابِهِ الطَّيِّبِينَ

Translators' Introduction

THE Book on the *Mysteries of Purification* is the third book of the first quarter of *The Revival of the Religious Sciences* (*Iḥyāʾ ʿulūm al-dīn*); the first quarter of which focuses on formal worship. This book is the first of five books in this quarter which deal principally with questions of how to perform the formal acts of devotion that constitute the 'five pillars' (*al-arkān al-khamsa*) of the religion: the testimony of faith, the prayer, *zakat*, fasting, and pilgrimage. All of these are presented largely from the standpoint of the Shāfiʿī school of jurisprudence (*fiqh*), of which al-Ghazālī was probably the greatest authority of his day.[1]

1 The first of the five pillars, the testimony of faith, is the subject of Book 2 of this quarter, *The Principles of the Creed*. Books 3 and 4, on purification and the prayer itself, could be said to be two dimensions of the second pillar, prayer, and books 5, 6, and 7 treat *zakat*, fasting, and the pilgrimage. Purity is also mentioned briefly in book 7 of the second quarter, *The Proprieties of Travel*.

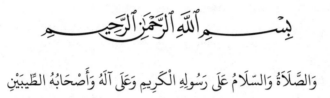

General Arrangement

In the Arabic version upon which this translation is based (Jedda: Dār al-Minhāj, 2011), *The Mysteries of Purification* occupies just over seventy pages.

The book begins with an introduction to the general question of purity, in which al-Ghazālī explains the *ḥadīth* "Purification is half of faith," and reminds the reader that, for the earliest Muslims, inner purification was much more important than outer purification. This occupies the first ten pages of the book.

The next twenty-four pages are devoted to an exposition of the ablution (*wuḍuʾ*), beginning with a lengthy explanation of what is considered pure water according to the Shāfiʿī school and ending with some sayings about the particular merits of the ablution

This is followed by two short explanations of how to perform the greater ablution (*ghusl*) and the ablution without water (*tayammum*); each of these is about two pages in length.

The final section of the book deals with the two general classes of substances that should or must be removed from the body. This section runs just over thirty pages, seven of which are devoted to the manners and use of the bathhouse (*ḥammām*) and ten of which discuss what is recommended and disapproved concerning the beard.

The Rite of Ablution in Islam

As the outline above indicates, the largest portion of this book deals with the physical rite of ablution (*wuḍūʾ*): its conditions, method, and object. This rite itself is based on two verses in the Qurʾān, 4:43 and 5:6. The latter of these two, which reiterates and expands upon the former, states:

> *O you who have believed, when you rise to* [*perform*] *prayer, wash your faces and your forearms to the elbows and wipe over your heads and wash your feet to the ankles. And if you are in a state of janaba, then purify yourselves. But if you are ill or on a journey or one of you comes from the place of relieving*

> *himself or you have contacted women and do not find water, then seek clean earth and wipe over your faces and hands with it. God does not intend to make difficulty for you, but He intends to purify you and complete His favor upon you that you may be grateful* (5:6).

Although the language of this verse is simple and straightforward, questions of how, exactly, this commandment was to be carried out arose almost immediately after its revelation. Initially, these were answered by eyewitness reports of what the Prophet himself did or guided others to do. With the passage of time, however, differences in these reports or in the way they were understood became the basis of *fiqh*, a word that has come to be translated as "jurisprudence," but which actually means, simply, "understanding."[2] By the middle of the third/ninth century, variations in *fiqh*—minor though they might be—were codified into the four main schools (*madhāhib*) of Sunnī Islam, the Ḥanafī, Shāfiʿī, Mālikī, and Ḥanbalī; each named after their founders.[3]

Beyond questions of *fiqh*, however, the simple act of ablution, ordained by the Qurʾān as a condition for the prayer and therefore an absolute obligation of the religion, had a tremendous impact on Islamic culture and on the lives of Muslims, be they male or female, young or old. Along with the prayer (*ṣalat*) itself, the ablution is the rite that an average Muslim repeats most often throughout his or her life—well over a hundred thousand times by some reckoning—and it is this rite, according to Muslim belief, by which any lawful act, be it an intrinsically devotional one such as reading the Qurʾān, or an

---

2 Fakhr al-Dīn al-Razī's *al-Tafsīr al-kabīr* (Beirut: Dār Iḥyāʾ al-Turāth al-ʿArabī, n.d.) which sums up all the questions that have arisen in respect to nearly every verse of the Qurʾān, presents no fewer than eighty questions on these 120 or so words. Some simple examples are the following: since the verse says "*when you rise to [perform] prayer*" does this mean that ablution has to be made any time one intends to offer the prayer or only under certain conditions? If someone is on a journey and stops somewhere along the way, how many days may they spend in that place and still be considered a traveler? Do the words, "contact with women" mean any physical contact between a man and woman or only sexual contact?" What, precisely, constitutes "clean high ground?"

3 An analogous situation exists in Shīʿī jurisprudence based on the teachings of the Shīʿī *imāms*.

ordinary human habit such as retiring to bed, may be considered worship.

It is largely in relation to this rite and the general rules of purity that traditional Muslim culture developed its own distinctive ways to clothe the human body. Arising from the simple *ridā* and *izār*, the top and bottom wraps worn by the earliest Muslims,[4] were loose-fitting pantaloons, long shirts, the *jalabiyya*, and similar garments which permit the position prescribed when visiting the stations of nature and cleansing thereafter, as well as the bowing, kneeling, and prostration of the prayer. Sandals or slippers and head coverings that are easy to remove and replace when the feet and head are cleansed come under this same category.

It was this rite that also provided the impetus behind the development of systems to supply running water for mosques and individual homes, and to the public baths for the greater ablution (*ghusl*). Historically, one of the marks of true civilization for a traditional Muslim city—besides the number of its gates, libraries, mosques, marketplaces, and gardens—was the number of its public baths. The great city of Cordoba, for example, at the height of its glory in the fourth/tenth century, was said to have seven hundred mosques and nine hundred public baths,[5] and it is interesting to note that when the Church sought to reassert its authority in Spain in the years following the fall of Granada in 1492, as the Inquisition loomed on the horizon, one of the first things it focused on was the prohibition and finally the destruction of public baths.[6]

---

4 These are the obligatory clothes in which the pilgrimage is performed.

5 Stanley Lane-Poole, *The Moors in Spain* (New York: G. Putnam Sons, 1903), 136.

6 The Proclamation of Toledo (1514) forbade the lighting of public baths on Fridays, feast days, and Sundays, the latter presumably because recently converted Moriscos were so ingrained with the habit of ablution before worship that they would do so even to attend the Sunday Mass. Ten years earlier, the Oran *fatwā* was issued to give the Muslims in Spain who were trying to cling to their religion remarkable licenses vis a vis the greater and lesser ablution and the prayer. See L. P. Harvey, *Muslims in Spain, 1500 to 1614* (Chicago: University of Chicago Press, 2005), 52, and 61. Philip II (d. 1598) eventually ordered that the baths of Cordova be destroyed, but the Mozarab "problem" persisted in Spain until 1609, when his son, Philip III, ordered the expulsion of all remaining Muslims from the Iberian Peninsula.

Purification of the Body and the "Physicality" of Islam

Besides what might be called the political reasons that the fifteenth- and sixteenth-century Church suppressed the rite of ablution, was the perception that also existed at the time (and still exists to some extent) that questions of the body, impurity, grooming, and bathing are somehow antithetical to spirituality and part of what might be called the "physicality" of Islam.[7] Certainly, no other major religion includes among its scriptural sources narrations about how its founder and those around him carried out basic human functions, how they approached sexuality not only as a means of procreation but also as a source of pleasure for both sexes, and how women dealt with their menstrual cycles and childbirth. According to a certain understanding of religion, a man or woman of God should be beyond such questions and, as the Qurʾān relates, even some pagan Arabs asked about the Prophet Muḥammad, *What is this messenger that eats food and walks in the markets? Why was there not sent down to him an angel so he would be with him a warner?* [25:7].

The Qurʾānic response to this kind of question—*If there were upon the earth angels walking securely, We would have sent down to them from the heaven an angel* [*as a*] *messenger* [17:95]—means, according traditional commentaries, that a messenger of revelation to human beings must himself be human, that is, the one who comes with a revelation described as "all-encompassing,"[8] must himself be someone who enters into and experiences the totality of the human state, including the needs, desires, strengths, infirmities, pleasures, and pains of the human body.[9] Moreover, the general Islamic conception

7 This same argument has been raised concerning the Qurʾānic descriptions of heaven as a place where what are apparently sensual pleasures will be enjoyed. It is beyond the scope of this introduction to deal with how these descriptions may be understood literally, apart from citing the saying of the Prophet, "God has prepared for His faithful servants in heaven what no eye has ever seen, no ear has ever heard, and no human heart has ever imagined," which appears in the collections of Muslim and al-Bukhārī as well as in nearly all of the other main collections.

8 As the Prophet is quoted as having said in the *ḥadīth*: "I have been given the all-encompassing word." al-Bukhārī, 7013; Muslim, 523.

9 "...It was the destiny of Muhammad to penetrate with exceptional versatility into

of the body, its senses, and even its sexuality, is not that they are obstacles to spirituality, but rather that they are among God's signs in creation, and therefore they possess the potential to be vehicles of worship and reasons for gratitude: *He created the heavens and earth in truth and formed you and perfected your forms; and to Him is the [final] destination* [64:3]; *And God has extracted you from the wombs of your mothers not knowing a thing, and He made for you hearing and vision and intellect that perhaps you would be grateful* [16:78]; *And of His signs is that He created for you from yourselves mates that you may find tranquility in them; and He placed between you affection and mercy* [30:21].

This same perspective helps explain the apparently disparate elements in the Prophet's saying: "In this world, women and perfume have been made beloved for me, and the coolness of my eye has been placed in the prayer."[10]

The "Mysteries" of Purification

This interplay between the formal and spiritual is undoubtedly among the "mysteries" or "secrets" (*asrār*) contained in the rites of purification and is implicit throughout this book and the entirety of the *Iḥyāʾ ʿulūm al-dīn*. For al-Ghazālī, however, the mysteries that matter most are not theoretical, conceptual, or esoteric, but rather those that help deepen actual practice. As he writes at the beginning of the *Book of Knowledge*:

> This work will deal only with the science of [proper] conduct, and not with [spiritual] unveiling, which one is not permitted to record in writing, although it is the ultimate aim of saints and the ultimate aim of the sincere. The science of [proper]

---

the domain of human experience, both public and private.... [He] was not only shepherd, merchant, hermit, exile, soldier, law-giver and prophet-priest-king; he was also an orphan... for many years the husband of one wife much older than himself, a many times bereaved father, a widower, and finally the husband of many wives, some much younger than himself." Martin Lings, *What is Sufism?* (Berkeley and Los Angeles: University of California Press, 1975), 34 and note 1.

10 Al-Nasāʾī, 7:61; Ibn Ḥanbal, 3:128.

> conduct is merely a path that leads to unveiling and only through that path did the prophets of God communicate with the people and lead them to Him. Concerning [spiritual] unveiling, the prophets عَلَيْهِمُ ٱلسَّلَامُ spoke only figuratively and briefly through signs and symbols, because they realized the inability of people's mind to comprehend..[11]

For Imām al-Ghazālī, the greatest concern in the *Book on the Mysteries of Purification* is that these rites, as well as other actions relating to the cleanliness and grooming of the body, be accomplished as perfectly as possible, which means combining formal correctness with inner presence. It is to aid the worshiper toward this goal that he intersperses passages of Shāfiʿī *fiqh* with the supplications that the Prophet صَلَّى ٱللَّهُ عَلَيْهِ وَسَلَّمَ or those made by the Companions as they carried out these actions, comments about the meaning behind them, and offers insights into what the heart's intention should be in carrying them out. In short, the "mysteries of purification" are the keys that may help a worshiper reach an ever-deeper realization that everything in the formal, temporal realm is a reflection of some reality in the spiritual and eternal realm. This is summed up nowhere so beautifully and succinctly as in this passage, which occurs toward the end of this book:

> So it is with the traveler on the path of the hereafter: he sees nothing of things except what will teach him and remind [him] of the hereafter. In all that he looks upon, God opens for him a way to learn from it. Thus, if he beholds something black, he is reminded of the darkness of the grave; if he sees a snake, it recalls to his mind the vipers of hell; if he beholds something ugly and repulsive, he is reminded of Munkar, Nakīr, and the guardians of hell (*al-zabāniyya*); if he hears a frightening sound, he is reminded of the sounding of the horn [that will signal the Last Day]; and likewise, if he sees something beautiful, he remembers the bliss of heaven, and if he hears a word of rejection or acceptance in the marketplace or at home,

---

11 Al-Ghazālī, *The Book of Knowledge*, trans. Kenneth Honerkamp (Louisville, KY: Fons Vitae, 2015), xlv.

it reminds him that in the end, after the reckoning, all that he accomplished [in life] will be either rejected or accepted.

Passages from the *Qūt al-Qulūb*

As with a number of other books of *Iḥyāʾ ʿulūm al-dīn*, *The Mysteries of Purification* contains passages taken verbatim or with slight alteration from the *Qūt al-qulūb* of the earlier Shāfiʿī Sufi scholar, Abū Ṭālib al-Makki (d. 386/996). In describing how to perform the greater and lesser ablution, for example, al-Ghazālī quotes section 33 of the *Qūt al-qulūb*, "Dhikr daʿāʾim al-islām al-khams" [On the five supports of Islām].[12] The discussion about grooming the beard which ends this book of the *Iḥyāʾ ʿulūm al-dīn* comes largely from section 36 of the *Qūt al-qulūb*, "Fī faḍāʾil ahl al-sunna" [On the excellence of the people of the *sunna*],[13] and the passages about the manners related to the bathhouse are taken largely from section 46 of the *Qūt al-qulūb*, "Kitāb dhikr dukhūl al-ḥammām" [The book on entering the bathhouse].[14] In addition, the end of section 31, "Mā aḥdath al-nās min al-qawl wa-l-fiʿl" [What was innovated of speech and acts], explains certain innovations in speech and deeds that relate to the bathhouse and are counted among the disapproved innovations that appeared in the fourth-/tenth-century Baghdad of Abū Ṭālib al-Makkī.[15] It was Imām al-Ghazālī's particular genius to be able to build these passages and others into the amazing and monumental architecture of *The Revival of the Religious Sciences*.

Our Work

This translation is based on the new edition of the *Iḥyāʾ ʿulūm al-dīn* published in 2011 by Dār al-Minhāj, Jedda, in commemoration of the

12 Abū Ṭālib al-Makkī, *Qūt al-qulūb*, 2:83.
13 Abū Ṭālib al-Makkī, *Qūt al-qulūb*, 2:138.
14 Abū Ṭālib al-Makkī, *Qūt al-qulūb*, 2:259.
15 Abū Ṭālib al-Makkī, *Qūt al-qulūb*, 1:163.

nine-hundredth anniversary of the passing from this world of the Imām, Abū l-Ḥāmid al-Ghazālī (d. 505/1111). Besides this beautifully printed and edited work, we depended heavily on the first volume of the ten-volume commentary on the *Iḥyāʾ ʿulūm al-dīn*, the *Itḥāf al-sādat al-muttaqīn fī sharḥ Iḥyāʾ ʿulūm al-dīn* by Murtaḍā l-Zabīdī (d. 1205/1791). An earlier translation into English of this part of the *Iḥyāʾ ʿulūm al-dīn* by Nabih Faris, first published in Pakistan in 1961, and reprinted in 1991, has also been a useful reference.

Acknowledgments

Our deepest thanks go first to Gray Henry, director of Fons Vitae, for her vision. In addition, our gratitude goes to those who are guiding this project at Fons Vitae: Muhammad Hozien, who also provides the comprehensive and beneficial website of al-Ghazālī works; to Valerie Joy Turner for editing and indexing the English; to the unknown donor by whose generosity we received, literally on our doorstep, the ten volumes of the new edition, at the time unavailable in Morocco; to Hamza Yusuf and Abdal Hakim Winter for the advice and inspiration they have lent to the al-Ghazālī project; to our colleague and friend at the Center for Language and Culture, Marrakesh, Sidi Brahim Zoubairi, for reading the final manuscript and offering extremely useful suggestions; and always and ever, to our families for their patience, love, and support.

In the Name of God, the Merciful and Compassionate
Book 3 of the *Revival of the Religious Sciences*
Kitāb asrār al-ṭahāra

The Mysteries of Purification

It is composed of four chapters[1]

Chapter 1: On Purification from Impurities (*khabath*): What Is to be Removed, What may be Used to Remove It, and the Way It Is to be Removed

Chapter 2: Purification from the Occurrences that Remove Purity (*aḥdāth*): The Lesser Ablution (*wuḍū͗*), the Greater Ablution (*ghusl*), the Ablution without Water (*tayammum*)

Chapter 3: Cleaning What Adds to the Body Externally, of Which There Are Two Basic Kinds: The External and What Grows from the Body; and the External Consisting of Forms of Dirt and Secretions, of Which There Are Eight

Chapter 4: Practices That Are Disapproved of Concerning the Beard

1 The text of this page was compiled from Imām al-Ghazālī's chapter titles. The original text does not have a list of contents.

[Author's Introduction]

PRAISE be to God who, in kindness to His servants, ordained cleanliness (*naẓāfa*) as part of their worship, poured down upon their hearts His light and grace to purify their souls, and made water, limpid and gentle, for the cleansing of their bodies.

May the blessing of God be upon Muḥammad and his people, good and pure, by whom guidance flooded into the farthest reaches of the world, a blessing that will shelter us with its benediction on the fearful day and be a shield raised between us and every calamity and disaster.

To proceed, the Prophet ﷺ said, "Religion (*dīn*) is built upon cleanliness,"[1] and also, "Purity (*ṭahara*) is the key to prayer."[2] And God most high says, *Within it are men who love to purify themselves, and God loves those who purify themselves* [9:108]. And the Prophet ﷺ also said, "Purification is half of faith,"[3] and God most high says, *God does not intend to make difficulty for you, but He intends to purify you...* [5:6].

People of insight (*dhū l-baṣāʾir*) have understood from the outward (*ẓahir*, pl. *ẓawāhir*) [meaning] of these sayings that the most important matter is inward (*sirr*, pl. *sarāʾir*) purification of the

1 Narrated by al-Rāfiʿī in his history, *al-Tadwīn fī akhbār Qazwīn*, 1:176, with wording close to this. In al-Tirmidhī, *al-Jāmiʿ al-ṣaḥīḥ*, 2799 (hereafter references to al-Tirmidhī are to this work, unless otherwise noted), we find the wording, "Truly, God is pure and loves what is pure; is clean and loves cleanliness. . ."

2 Abū Dāwūd, 61; al-Tirmidhī, 3; Ibn Māja, 275.

3 Al-Tirmidhī, 3519.

soul. Indeed, it is unlikely that when the Prophet صَلَّى ٱللَّٰهُ عَلَيْهِ وَسَلَّمَ said, "Purification (*ṭahara*) is half of faith," he meant [only] cleansing the body with a stream of water, while leaving the heart to ruin in refuse and filth. Such is absurd to even imagine.

There are, in fact, four levels (*rutba*, pl. *marātib*) of purification.

The first level is to purify the body from occurrences [which void the ablution],[4] from substances considered impure, and from [certain natural] growths and excretions.

The second level is to purify the members of the body from transgression and sin.

The third level is to purify the heart from immoral character [traits] and baseness.

The fourth level is to purify the innermost being from all that is not God most high, this being the purification of the prophets and saints.

At each of these levels, purification is half of practice. The ultimate goal of practice relating to the innermost being, for example, is the unveiling of God's majesty and grandeur. But this [divine] gnosis (*maʿrifa*) cannot truly dwell there as long as what is other than God has not departed. Thus, God says, *Say, "God* [revealed it]." *Then leave them* [6:91], for they cannot co-exist in one heart. *And God has not made for a man two hearts in his interior.* [33:4].

At the level of the heart, the ultimate goal of practice is for the heart to be filled with virtue and orthodoxy, but this is not possible until it is cleansed of vice and heterodoxy, and so to rid it of these latter is the first of two halves and a condition for the second. In this sense, purification of the heart is half of faith, just as the first of two halves is purification of the limbs of the body from what is unclean (*manāhī*) [lit. what is forbidden], while the second is for the limbs to be filled with worship.

Such are the stations (*maqāmāt*) of faith. For each station, there is a level (*ṭabaqa*) and a servant (*ʿabd*) of God will not reach a level that is higher except by surpassing one that is lower. He will not reach the level of purifying the innermost being from blameworthy traits and filling it with those which are praiseworthy until he has

---

4 *Aḥdath*, literally "occurrences," are generally understood to be the passing of urine, feces, or bodily gas.

completed the purification of the heart from blameworthy character [traits] and filled it with praiseworthy character [traits], nor will he reach the latter until he has purified the members of the body from sins and filled them with devotion. The more precious and nobler the goal, the more difficult and longer the path, and the more filled with obstacles it will be. So, do not suppose that [the higher levels of purification] will be reached by mere wishful thinking or without effort.

Moreover, anyone whose vision is blinded to the differences between these levels will understand nothing of the degrees of purification except the lowest one, which is like the extreme outer husk compared to the sought-after kernel within. This kind of person will become totally focused on [physical purity], immersed in studying it, and spend all his time ridding his body of impurities, washing his clothes, cleaning himself, and looking for good sources of running water. He will imagine, either because of the whisperings of doubt[5] or some mental obsession, that this alone is the sought-after noble purity, and will remain ignorant of the lives of the early believers who devoted all their thought and care to the purification of their hearts but were, in fact, very lenient concerning the purity of the body.

Thus, even ʿUmar, with his high rank, made the ablution with water from a Christian woman's earthen jar,[6] and the [other early

---

5 *Waswasa*, literally, "whispering." In the first book of the third quarter of the *Iḥyāʾ ʿulūm al-dīn*, *On the Marvels of the Heart*, al-Ghazālī defines "whisperings" as those suggestions that lead to evil and originate with the devil. He mentions a *ḥadīth* that appears in the *Sunan* of al-Bayhaqī, that "The ablution has a devil named al-Walahān. Beware of him!" or in another narration, ". . . and beware of whisperings about [the purity of] water." Quoted along with this in the same book of the *Iḥyāʾ ʿulūm al-dīn* is another *ḥadīth* in which ʿUthmān b. Abī l-ʿĀṣ is reported to have said to the Prophet ﷺ, "The devil has come between me and my prayer and recitation." To which the Prophet ﷺ replied, "That is a devil named Khinzibun. If you sense him near you, take refuge in God and spit thrice to the left." See *Iḥyāʾ ʿulūm al-dīn* (Jedda: Dār al-Minhāj, 2011), 5:97–99 and the current work, 33.

6 Al-Bayhaqī, *al-Sunan al-kubra*, 1:32, where this incident is related in detail, including the fact that after making the ablution, ʿUmar رضي الله عنه asked to see the elderly Christian woman whose young daughter had brought him water; he called her to become a Muslim, which she did. "Whereupon, she uncovered her head—and her hair was pearly white—and said, 'Now I can die,' upon which ʿUmar said, 'O God,

believers], rather than washing their hands from fat and morsels of food, would wipe them on the arches of their feet, considering potash[7] (ʿ*ushnān*) an innovation [to be avoided]. These first Muslims also offered the prayer in mosques with earthen floors and walked the roads barefoot. The greatest among them were people who slept with nothing between them and the ground, who wiped themselves with nothing more than dry stones.

Abū Hurayra رَضِيَٱللَّهُعَنْهُ and others among the people of the bench[8] said: "We would be eating grilled meat and the time of prayer would come upon us, so we would wipe our hands on the pebbles around us, rub them with dry earth, and utter the *takbīr*."[9]

And ʿUmar رَضِيَٱللَّهُعَنْهُ said, "In the time of God's Messenger, may the blessings of God and peace be upon him, we had no knowledge of potash. Our towels were the arches of our feet and if we ate something oily, that is how we wiped our hands."[10]

It was also said, "The first innovations to appear after [the time of] God's Messenger, may the blessings of God and peace be upon him, were four things: the use of sieves, potash, tables, and satiety."

What they cared most about was to be inwardly clean, even to the extent that some of them said,

> It is better to offer the prayer in sandals! When the Messenger of God removed his sandals in the prayer, [it was because] Gabriel عَلَيْهِٱلسَّلَامُ had informed him that there was something unclean on them. But then, when the people proceeded to

---

I bear witness to this!'" This incident is also referred to in al-Bukhārī, 193, in the narration by ʿAbdallāh b. ʿUmar: "Men and women used to make their ablution together in the time of the Prophet, upon whom be peace."

7 ʿ*Ushnān* is a plant belonging to the moss family; the Arabs burned it to make potash or alkali. The alkali, sodium hydroxide, is still an essential ingredient in the making of soap.

8 The people of the bench (*ahl al-ṣuffa*) were the poorest of those who immigrated from Mecca to Medina; when there was no work or sustenance to be found, they spent their days in the shaded part of the entrance to the first mosque. Among them number some of the greatest of the Companions.

9 Ibn Māja, 3311, with wording close to this. The *takbīr*, the formula *Allāhu akbar* (God is greater), is the utterance that begins the prayer.

10 Abū Ṭālib al-Makkī, *Qūt al-qulūb*, 2:142.

remove their sandals as well, he asked them, "Why are you taking off your sandals?"[11]

Al-Nakhaʿī so disapproved of those who removed their sandals [for prayer] that he once said, "I wish some needy person would come and take them all!"[12]

Such was their lenience toward these matters that they would walk barefoot down muddy roads, sit in them, pray directly on the earthen floors of mosques, and eat flour made from wheat and barley upon which animals had trodden and urinated. They did not try to avoid the sweat of camels and horses even though these animals regularly roll in impurities [urine and dung], nor has there been a single question recorded from any of them asking about the details of what constitutes impure substances. Such was their leniency toward these matters.

Yet in this present age[13] there has appeared a group who call their folly cleanliness and say, "This is the foundation of religion!" They spend most of their time in beautifying themselves outwardly, like a hairdresser grooming a bride, while inwardly they are in ruin, full of pride, conceit, ignorance, ostentation, and hypocrisy, and they neither disapprove of these [faults] nor even wonder about them. But were someone to wipe [themselves] clean[14] with nothing more than a stone, or walk the earth barefoot, or pray upon bare ground or directly on the reed mats in a mosque without first spreading out a prayer rug, or walk across a carpeted area without socks lest their feet shed skin, or perform the ablution out of the pot of an old woman or an irreligious man, all of them would rise up against him, reproach him severely, label him dirty (*qadhir*), expel him from their midst, and disdain from eating or mixing with him. Indeed, they call an ascetic appearance, which [the Prophet described as] "a part of faith," filthiness[15] and their folly [they call] cleanliness. Then

11 Abū Dāwūd, 650; Ibn Ḥanbal, 3:20.

12 Ibn Abī Shayba, 7964.

13 By which he means around 490/1100.

14 The word *istinjāʾ* refers to wiping after defecation.

15 Abū Dāwūd, 4161, with the wording, "Do you not hear? Do you not hear? To be ragged and disheveled is a part of faith." In the context, this means that someone who looks this way should not be thought of as outside the community of believers.

behold how what is wrong is considered right, and what is right is considered wrong![16] Behold how the outward form of religion has been lost even as its essential truth and knowledge were also lost.

If you then ask me, "Are you saying that the habits that Sufis have instituted concerning their appearance and cleanliness are wrong and should be avoided?" I would answer, "God forbid that I should make a blanket pronouncement." But I would say, concerning this [kind of] cleanliness and excessive care, the preparation of vessels and tools, the wearing of foot coverings and clothes against the dust, and other similar habits, that they are permissible if they are considered purely in themselves, and if they are considered in connection to certain spiritual states and intentions, then they may sometimes be right, sometimes wrong.

As for considering them permissible in themselves, this is obvious: if someone who keeps these practices is dealing with his own possessions, his own body, and his own clothes, then let him do whatever he wants as long as it is not wasteful or excessive.

These [practices] become wrong, however, if the one who observes them makes them the very principle of religion, if he thinks that they are applications of the Prophet's saying ﷺ: "Religion is built upon cleanliness,"[17] and then criticizes anyone who is lenient in these matters, like the early believers were. [They are also wrong] if the one who does them does so in order to appear a certain way to people, so that they might consider him good. Such is [simply] ostentation and should be avoided. Under these two conditions, [these practices] are disapproved.

They are good and acceptable, however, when the one who observes them does so for a good purpose, and does not criticize others for not doing them, nor delays offering the prayer at its earliest time because of them, nor becomes diverted by them from accomplishing deeds which are better, or from learning and teaching,

---

16 Referring to a *ḥadīth* in al-Ṭabarānī, *al-Muʿjam al-awsaṭ*, 11381, and *al-Muʿjam al-kabīr*, 715, and also by Ibn Abī l-Dunyā, 32, in which the Prophet ﷺ asked some Companions, "How will you be when you see your youth sunk in licentiousness and your women become tyrants?" They asked, "Will that happen?" He replied, "Worse than that. How will you be when you see what is right considered wrong, and what is wrong considered right?"

17 See footnote 1, above.

and so forth. If their observance is free from all this, then they are permissible and may even be a way of drawing nearer to God by way of good intention.

Such practice, however, is not easy for anyone except the idle class, who, if they were not busy spending their time doing this, would spend it sleeping or chatting about what does not concern them. For them, a preoccupation with physical cleanliness is better, for it renews for them the remembrance of God and the remembrance of acts of worship (*ʿibādāt*). As such, there is nothing wrong with this as it causes neither harm nor waste.

For the people of knowledge and practice, however, it is not fitting to spend time [with outward purification] beyond what is necessary. For them, to go beyond this would be wrong and a waste of this life, which is the rarest and most precious of jewels to the one who can use it beneficially. No one should wonder at this, for the good deeds of those of the pious are the faults of the saintly.

It is not fitting for someone of the idle class to abandon [all concern with] cleanliness, find fault with the Sufis who practice it, and [then] claim that they are imitating the Companions. The Companions had little to do with this only because they had more important things to accomplish. Thus, when it was asked of Dāwūd al-Ṭāʾī, "Why do you not tend your beard?" He answered, "[Do you think] I have any free time?"[18]

For this reason, I do not consider it right for a scholar, or a student, or worker[19] to waste his time washing his clothes so as to avoid wearing clothes washed with bleach [in a public laundry] because he imagines that bleaching is less [pure] than washing. Those of the earliest days [of Islam] would offer their prayers wearing tanned hides, and not one of them is known to have made any distinction between what is bleached and what is tanned, in terms of what is pure or impure.[20] Yes, they would avoid impurity

18 Abū Nuʿaym, *Ḥilya*, 7:339.

19 *ʿĀmil*; this could be understood as someone who has to work or someone deeply involved in devotional practices.

20 Some people considered bleaching and tanning impure, because they involved the use of questionable substances. Bleach was seen as similar to soap, which some considered an innovation (as mentioned above). At that time, the process of tanning leather included soaking it in animal urine to soften it.

if they saw it, but they would not try to discover [all] the minute possibilities [of what constitutes purity]. They did, however, reflect deeply upon the subtle details of what constitutes ostentation and injustice, which is why Sufyān al-Thawrī, for example, once said to a companion who was walking with him and looked at a particularly ornate door of a house, "Do not do that! If people did not look at it, its owner would not have gone to such excess! Looking at it only encourages him to excess!"[21]

It was to discover these kinds of subtleties that they used the power of their minds, not in figuring out what might possibly be impure.

Thus, if a scholar can find a common person to whom he can give the job of washing his clothes, it is generally better. It is good from the standpoint of being lenient [about questions of purity]. It is also beneficial for that common person to be given this work because it will occupy his lower self with something permissible, and as long as it is thus occupied, it will be kept from sin. Indeed, if the lower self is not kept busy, it will keep the one who possesses it busy instead. And if that common person wishes to be closer to the scholar, then [working for him in this way] is one of the best means of doing so.

Indeed, the scholar's time is too precious to be spent with such things, so [time] should be preserved, while the most precious time for a common person is in doing such work and he will derive from it goodness in every respect of the word.

Let this example serve as a model when considering all other activities, ordering them by merit, and giving priority to some over others: paying attention to the details of how to reckon the moments of life and use them for what is best is more important than paying attention to the details of the wealth of this world in its entirety.

If you have understood this introduction and seen that purification has four levels, then know that in this book we shall speak only of the fourth [level], namely, outward purification, since in this first half [of the *Iḥyāʾ ʿulūm al-dīn*], we are only concerned with the outward aspects [of worship].

---

21 Abū Ṭālib al-Makkī, *Qūt al-qulūb*, 1:170.

We say, therefore, that there are three parts to outward purity: purification from unclean substances (*khabath*), purification from occurrences (*ḥadath*) that void the ablution, and purification from what grows naturally from the body and may be removed by clipping the nails, shaving, using a depilatory, circumcision, and so forth.

1

On Purification from Impurities (*khabath*): What Is to be Removed, What may be Used to Remove It, and the Way It Is to be Removed

Part 1: What Is to be Removed—Impurities Are of Three Sources: Inanimate [Things], Living Creatures, and Parts of Living Creatures

All inanimate substances are considered pure except wine and other intoxicating drinks.

All animate creatures are pure except the dog, the pig, and whatever is born from one or both of them.[1] When animate creatures die, however, all of them are impure except five: human beings, fish, locusts, apple worms, and similarly, any creature that does not alter food [and] does not have regularly circulating blood. This would include flies, beetles, and the like. If creatures such as these fall into water, the water remains pure.

Substances that are part of living beings fall into two categories. The first is whatever has been cut from a living being, in which case its ruling is the same as what applies to what is dead. Hair that is

1 That is, the offspring of a dog mating with another species of the Canidae family or hybrid breeds of pig.

cut or dies [and falls out], however, does not become impure, while bone does.

The second category comprises the wet substances which emerge from within the body. If these do not naturally collect in a certain place [in the body], as is the case with tears, sweat, saliva, and mucus from the nose [which do collect in one location, but are gathered there as the body needs them], then they are pure. But if they normally and regularly collect in a particular place, they are impure. The exception to this is the substance of life: semen and egg.

Therefore, substances such as the pus, blood, excrement, and urine of all living creatures are all impure.

Of the impurities mentioned, nothing is excepted, whether in great or small quantities, except for five things, [as follows].

The first is the trace of excrement that does not go beyond the anus; this is [sometimes] left after wiping with stones.[2]

The second is the soil and dust of roads, even though it surely contains impurities; [it is exempted] to the extent that it is impossible to avoid. This does not apply, however, to someone [whose garments are] soiled and simply makes no effort or fails [to clean them].

The third is what may remain on the soles of foot coverings (*khuff*), after attempting to rub off whatever can be rubbed off, from what is always in the roads.[3]

The fourth is blood from fleas, whether it be a tiny amount or more, unless it goes beyond the normal limits, be it on your own clothes or someone else's [clothes] that you are wearing.

The fifth is blood, pus, or other discharge that comes from pimples. Once Ibn ʿUmar رَضِيَ اللَّهُ عَنْهُ rubbed a pimple on his face and blood came out of it, but he offered the prayer without washing.[4]

Similarly, what might seep from a persistent boil or from a scar left after bloodletting [is considered pure]. If [this sort of discharge or bleeding] occurs rarely, however, then it is regarded like menstrual

2 Before the use of toilet paper, smooth, dry stones were used for wiping. This practice continues in many rural areas of Muslim countries.

3 Al-Ghazālī is referring to a time when animals and humans shared the same roads. If either animal or human excrement were to get on the soles of one's foot coverings, specifically the leather "sock" known as *khuff*, whatever could not be rubbed off is excused.

4 Al-Bayhaqī, *al-Sunan al-kubrā*, 1:141.

blood and not in the category of pimples, from which human beings are never totally free.

The fact that the law (*sharʿ*) excuses these five categories of impurity should show you that the question of purity is based on leniency and that the innovations concerning it are simply whisperings of doubt (*waswasa*) with no foundation.

Part 2: On the Solid and Liquid Substances Used to Remove Impurities

In respect to what is solid [this is generally taken to mean] the stone used for wiping and drying bodily excretion. [Whatever is used for this process] must be something pure in itself, able to cleanse, and not something which will spread the excretion.[5] It must be solid [not crumbling], pure, absorbent, and may not be something reverenced.[6]

As for liquids, none may be used to cleanse away impurity except water, and specifically, water which itself is pure and untainted by being mixed with something with which it is not normally in contact.

Water loses its purity if its taste, color, or smell are altered by coming into contact with something impure. If [one of] these qualities has not been altered, however, and the quantity [of water] approaches two hundred and fifty *mann*, which is equal to five hundred *ruṭl* as measured in Iraq,[7] then it is not considered polluted, according to the saying of the Prophet ﷺ, "If the quantity of water reaches two water pots (*qullatayn*), it does not bear impurity."[8] If

5 Modern toilet paper fulfils all these conditions.

6 "Reverenced" (*muḥtaram*) in this context may mean, for example, a piece of dry bread that is reverenced because it is food. To this day, it is common practice in Muslim lands for one to pick up pieces of dry bread found on the ground and place them somewhere elevated, where a bird or small creature might eat it. It may also apply to anything with writing on it, especially if it includes the name of God, the prophets, or their words. Al-Zabīdī, *Itḥāf*, 2:322–323.

7 One *ruṭl* as al-Ghazālī uses it, is equal to approximately one pound. "Near" is explained as meaning one or two pounds more or less. Al-Zabīdī, *Itḥāf*, 2:323. In present-day measurements, this refers to about eight cubic feet of water.

8 Abū Dāwūd, 63, al-Tirmidhī, 67, al-Nasāʾī, 1:46, Ibn Māja, 517, and elsewhere. In this context the word *qulla*, here translated as "water pot," refers to a standing

it is less than that, however, then according to al-Shāfiʿī رضي الله عنه it is impure. All this concerns still water.

In the case of flowing water, if there is some alteration in [its three essential attributes] caused by contact with what is impure, then the current that has been altered is considered impure, but that which is above or below it [is not], since currents of water are separate from one another.

Similarly, if what is impure flows into a current of water, the place where it enters the water is considered impure as well as what is to the right or left of this place if the quantity of water is less than two full water pots. If the current of water is stronger than the current of any impurity flowing into it, then the water above it is pure while what is below it is polluted. This holds true even at some distance away and when the quantity of water is great. The exception to this is water that has collected in a [hand-dug] basin of which the quantity is [at least] two water pots.

If two water pots (or more) full of impure water collect [in a hand-dug basin or the like], then it is considered pure and does not lose its purity by being subsequently removed [from that basin].

These are the teachings of al-Shāfiʿī رضي الله عنه, and I would have preferred it had they been like those of Mālik رضي الله عنه—that water, even in a small quantity, does not become impure unless [its color, taste, or smell is] altered—for the need for water is pressing and the condition of there being at least two water pots opens people to whisperings of doubt (*waswasa*) and occasions hardship. Upon my life, this causes hardship, and anyone who has experienced it and thought about it will know what I saying.

Something I have no doubt about, however, is that if this condition [of two water pots had existed from the beginning], then the places where it would have made purification the most difficult to accomplish would have been Mecca and Medina, because of the scarcity of both flowing and still waters there.

Yet from the beginning of the time of the Messenger of God صلى الله عليه وسلم to the end of the time of his Companions رضي الله عنهم there is no recorded incident concerning purification nor question

---

water container generally made out of fired clay.

concerning how to keep water from becoming impure, even while the vessels used to hold it were handled by children and maidservants who pay no attention to impurities.

ʿUmar رضي الله عنه made the ablution with water in a Christian woman's earthenware jar.[9] This is a clear proof that for him the only thing that mattered concerning the purity of the water was the fact that its [three qualities were unaltered]. Otherwise, the impurity of the Christian woman and her vessel obviously would have outweighed anything else.

The difficulty in following the teachings [of al-Shāfiʿī in the condition of two water pots] and the absence of any questions about this [in those times] is one proof[10] and the action of ʿUmar رضي الله عنه another.

The third proof is that [it is recorded that] God's Messenger صلى الله عليه وسلم tilted a water vessel so that a female cat could drink from it and [the early believers] did not cover water vessels to prevent cats from drinking from them, even after having seen them eat mice, [because they know] that in their land there were no hand-dug basins where cats could drink, nor were they able to climb down into wells.[11]

The fourth [proof] is that al-Shāfiʿī رضي الله عنه stipulates that water in a tub used for washing something impure remains pure as long as it is not changed [in its three properties], but becomes impure if it is [changed]. What is the difference between water becoming impure because of being poured into something impure and water becoming impure because what is impure is poured into it? [And if there is no difference], then what is meant by saying, "The force by which the water flows repels impurity," even while this flow of water would not prevent its mixing with the impurity?

If [al-Shāfiʿī's] stipulation is based on the need [for water], then that same need should apply to [the opposite case]. There is no difference, then, between dumping [pure] water into a tub that

---

9 Al-Bayhaqī, *al-Sunan al-kubra*, 1:32, and see page 5, n.6.

10 That is, supporting the more lenient teachings of Imām Mālik in the question of water.

11 Which is to say that there was no other place where cats could drink. This is related in al-Daraquṭnī, 1:70, as something that was done by the famous Companion, Abū Qatāda رضي الله عنه.

contains some impure garments and dumping impure garments into a tub containing [pure] water, and both these things happen regularly when washing clothes or vessels.

The fifth proof is that [the early believers] would cleanse their private parts [after urination or defecation] near the edges of small currents of flowing water and there is no disagreement in the school of al-Shāfiʿī رَضِيَ ٱللَّهُ عَنْهُ, that if urine should fall into such flowing water and there is no change [in the water's three essential attributes], it is permissable to use that water for ablution, even when its quantity [i.e., of water] is small. What difference, then, is there between water that is flowing and water that is still?

Would that I knew whether the judgment in this matter is based on the absence of any alteration [in the water's attributes] or the force of its current, [and if the latter be true], then how far does this extend? Does it extend, for example, to the water that flows in the pipes (*anābīb*) of public baths or not? If not, then what is the difference? And if it does, then what is the difference between what might fall into them and what might fall into a stream of water from a vessel onto a body when in both cases the water is flowing?[12] Then, given the fact that urine mixes more freely with flowing water than a solid, fixed impurity does, if it is judged that what flows upon it, though unaltered [in color, taste, or smell], becomes impure except if is collected in a basin or container with a capacity of two water pots, then what is the difference between solid and liquid impurity when the water is one and the same and intermixing with something [impure] is certainly worse than [simply] being near it?[13]

Sixth, if a *ruṭl* of urine falls into [a quantity of water equal to] two full water pots[14] and then [that water] is divided into two

---

12 It is not clear from the text how impurities might fall into the pipes (*anābīb*) that carry water in the bathhouse. Al-Ghazālī might be referring to pipes made of fired clay which could have breaks along the top of the pipe or in places where they flowed through open canals.

13 Al-Iṣbahānī, quoted in al-Zabīdī, *Itḥāf*, says that according to an early opinion of al-Shāfiʿī, running water, whether it be little or much, fast flowing or slow, does not become polluted by contact with impurity unless one of its three attributes is altered. (al-Zabīdī, *Itḥāf*, 2:331).

14 A *ruṭl* is approximately one pint while two water pots are approximately 8 cubic feet of water.

portions, any water subsequently ladled out of those two portions is considered pure, even while it is known that [a] small amount of urine spreads throughout the water.

I wonder, therefore, whether the fact that it retains its purity is actually because of not being altered [in any one of the three attributes] or because of the strength of its large quantity, even after that quantity has been cut [in two] and removed and it is certain that some portion of the impurity is still in it?

Seventh is the fact that in times past, saintly and ascetic people continued to regularly perform their ablutions in public baths, putting their hands and ablution vessels into shared water basins, knowing that the quantity of water was small and that hands—both pure and impure—had repeatedly taken water from them.

These examples, along with the critical need [for water], strengthen in one's soul the conviction that the [faithful of times past] looked only for the absence of any change [in water's three attributes] as a sign of its purity, relying upon the saying of the Prophet ﷺ, "Water was created pure and nothing makes it impure except that which alters its taste, color, or smell."[15]

In this is an affirmation that it is in the nature of a liquid to transform to its own properties anything that might fall into it and be overwhelmed by its sheer quantity. You will see this [same principle] in the fact that if a dog happens to fall into a salt mine, it will be transformed into salt and be considered pure because of its transformation into salt and [its] loss of canine attributes [as the dog decomposes and becomes dust]. So, too, with vinegar or milk that might fall into water: if it is a small quantity, then its own attributes are lost and replaced with the attribute of water, and if a large quantity, it will predominate over the water and this predominance is known by a change in taste, color, or smell.

This is the standard to which the law (*sharʿ*) points in the question of water being strong enough [because of its current] to remove impurity, and it is worth relying on, for it will dispel the difficulties [that people face]. It also explains the meaning [of the *ḥadīth* that says] water is pure, and [the notion] that if it is in a greater quantity

15 Ibn Māja, 521, but without the words, "Water was created pure."

than something else, it will purify it. This is [also the standard that arises] in the matter of two water pots, the wash basin, running water, and also in tilting a water vessel so that a cat [might drink].

And do not suppose that these are examples of excusable exceptions. If such were the case, then water that comes into contact with the traces of excrement left after wiping, or with blood from a flea would become impure. [On the contrary], water does not become impure even when something impure is washed in it or cats drink from small quantities of it.

As for the saying of the Prophet صَلَّى ٱللَّٰهُ عَلَيْهِ وَسَلَّمَ, "It [water] does not carry impurity,'[16] this is difficult to understand, since water does carry impurity if it is changed [in color, taste or smell].

If it is said, "He meant [that it does not carry impurity] if it is not altered," then it could be said, "He meant that it is not ordinarily altered by the common impurities." Moreover, this necessarily means accepting that [it is] implicit [in the *ḥadīth*] that [the quantity of water in question] does not reach two full water pots. The suggestion that this *ḥadīth* has an implied meaning can be rejected based on less than the proofs we have mentioned.

The literal meaning of his saying, "[water] does not carry impurity" negates the act of carrying, which is [another way] to say that the water replaces the attributes [of impurity] with its own attributes, just as we might say, concerning the salt mine, "It does not carry [the attributes of] the dog or anything else [that falls into it]"; but rather transforms them into salt. And because people used to cleanse themselves after [urination or defecation] in the small streams of water and puddles left by rain, and they also dipped impure vessels in them, then [they] started to wonder if the water had been altered in its [essential attributes] or not, [so] he clarified [the situation by saying that] if the quantity of water reached two full water pots, it is not altered by the usual impurities.

And if you said that the Prophet صَلَّى ٱللَّٰهُ عَلَيْهِ وَسَلَّمَ said "Water does not carry impurity" but whenever the quantity of impurity becomes great, it does carry it, then the reasoning turns against you, for if the

16 See page 15, n. 8.

quantity of impurity becomes great, the water does carry it, both in a legal and a physical sense.

Thus, it is absolutely necessary that both the Shāfiʿī and Mālikī teachings specify "the ordinary impurities."

To sum up, my inclination in questions of impurity is toward leniency, based on my understanding of the way of the first believers and in order to eliminate the source of obsessions and doubts. For this reason, I offer this opinion (*fatwā*) on the differing views of purity.

Part 3: On the Ways of Removing Impurity

If the impurity is *ḥukmiyya* [that is, something judged to be present but] without a visible presence,[17] then it is enough to run water over all the places with which it may have come into contact.

If, on the other hand, it is *ʿayniyya* [that is, something which can be seen], then it must be physically removed, and in this case if a taste or color remains, the substance itself is still there, except for what adheres to another surface. If this cannot be removed by rubbing and scraping, it is excused.[18]

In respect to odor, if it remains, it indicates that the substance remains and it is not excused except in the case of something that has a very strong odor which is hard to remove. If it is scrubbed and squeezed out several times in succession, this takes the place of rubbing and scraping at a color. What removes doubts and suspicions [about these matters] is knowing with certitude that things have been created pure and if no impurity is perceived or known to be [on something or some place], then it may be used for the prayer and one should not try to find what quantity of impurity might be present.

---

17 Such as urine, which may have splattered on a surface but dried, leaving neither trace nor smell. Al-Zabīdī, *Itḥāf*, 2:334.

18 This is based on a *ḥadīth* of Khawla bt. Yasār, who said, "O Messenger of God صَلَّى ٱللَّهُ عَلَيْهِ وَسَلَّمَ I have only one garment and there is menstrual blood on it." He said, "When you have bathed yourself, then wash the place where the blood is and offer the prayer wearing it." I said, "And what if the spot will not come out?" He said, "It is enough that you have washed it with water. The spot will do you no harm." Abū Dāwūd, 365.

2

Purification from the Occurrences that Remove Purity (*aḥdāth*): The Lesser Ablution (*wuḍūʾ*), the Greater Ablution (*ghusl*), the Ablution without Water (*tayammum*)

We begin with how to cleanse the private parts after urination or defecation (*instinjāʾ*) and relate the order in which it is to be done, the correct manner in which to do it, and the elements considered *sunna*, beginning with the reasons for making the lesser ablution and the correct manner in which to answer the call of nature.

On the Manners Related to Answering the Call of Nature

If a person [is] out in the desert, he should remove himself some distance from the sight of onlookers and, if he can find [something], [he should] go behind it [to] cover himself. Also, he should not reveal his nakedness before getting to the place where he will squat. He should not face the sun or the moon, nor should he face or turn his back on the direction of prayer (*qibla*) except if [he is] inside a building. Even there, it is better if this can be avoided.

If he is in the desert it is permissible for him to screen himself with his mount or with the part of his garment that hangs down.

He should avoid squatting in a place where people gather to talk, or urinating into standing water, or under a fruit-bearing tree, or into burrows in the ground.

He should also avoid urinating where the ground is very hard or where a strong wind is blowing, so as not to splatter [his clothes].

He should squat mainly supported by his left foot, and if he enters a constructed toilet, he should do so with his left foot first and leave with his right foot first.

He should not urinate standing up. ʿĀʾisha رضي الله عنها said: "If anyone tells you that the Prophet صلى الله عليه وسلم used to urinate standing up, do not believe him!"[1] And ʿUmar رضي الله عنه said, "The Messenger of God صلى الله عليه وسلم once saw me urinate standing up and said to me, 'O ʿUmar, do not urinate standing up.'" ʿUmar said, "Thereafter, I never urinated standing up."[2] But there are circumstances in which it is permitted; Ḥudhayfa رضي الله عنه said, "[The Prophet] صلى الله عليه وسلم urinated standing up and then I brought him water for the lesser ablution and he performed it and then wiped his leather foot coverings (*khuffayhi*)."[3]

He should not urinate in the washroom.[4] The Prophet صلى الله عليه وسلم said, "Most of the doubts and suspicions [concerning purity] arise from this."[5] Ibn al-Mubārak, however, said, "If it has running water, there is no harm."[6]

He should not have anything with him upon which the name of God most high or His Messenger صلى الله عليه وسلم is written, nor should he enter the water closet bareheaded.

Upon entering, he should say, "In the name of God. I take refuge in God from abomination, impurity, corruption, and the corrupter, Satan the accursed,"[7] and upon leaving [he should say], "Praise be to God who removes from me what is harmful and leaves

---

1 Al-Tirmidhī, 12; al-Nasāʾī, 1:26; Ibn Māja, 307.

2 Al-Tirmidhī, 12; Ibn Māja, 308.

3 Muslim, 273, and al-Bukhārī, 224, but with no mention of wiping his foot coverings.

4 *Maghtasala*; in the context, this may be a room where the ablution is performed or clothes are washed.

5 Abū Dāwūd, 27; Ibn Māja, 304; al-Tirmidhī, 21; al-Nasāʾī, 1:19.

6 Al-Tirmidhī, 21.

7 Ibn Māja, 316 and Ibn Abī Shayba, 4. See the appendix.

in me what benefits me!"[8] [Both of these formula] are said outside the water closet.

He should also have the pebbles [to be used for wiping and drying] ready before squatting down and he should not wash with water in the same place where he has urinated or defecated.

A man should rid his member of any urine remaining on it by pressing and shaking it three times and checking with his hand at its end for moisture. But he should not think too much about whether [the urine was] completely expelled lest he becomes troubled [concerning purity] and burdened by this question. Let him consider that whatever [liquid] remains is water and if this bothers him, let him sprinkle some water there in order to be reassured and not let Satan control him with whisperings of doubt. According to a narration, the Prophet ﷺ sprinkled water following the ablution.[9] Thus, he who was the most knowledgeable of them all [concerning the rules of worship] carried this out in the lightest manner. Troubles and doubts about this, then, indicate a lack of understanding.

According to a *ḥadīth* narrated by Salmān رضي الله عنه, "The Messenger of God ﷺ taught us everything, even the way to pass excrement, and he told us not to wipe with bone or dried dung, nor to face the *qibla* while defecating or urinating."[10]

A man, arguing with one of the Companions who was a nomad, said, "I doubt that you even defecate the right way!" To which [the nomad] replied, "By your father! I certainly do! I certainly know the right way to do it! I go far from [where people's] footprints [appear in the sand], gather the pebbles [for wiping], and keep the *shīḥ* bushes in front of me and wind behind me. Then I squat (*iqʿāʾ*) like the gazelle, and raise (*ikhfāl*) my posterior like the ostrich."

The word *shīḥ* refers to the wormwood bush, an aromatic herb that grows in the desert. The word *iqʿāʾ* in this context means squatting, and *ikhfāl* means raising the posterior.

There is permission, however, for a person to urinate near someone else, as long as he screens himself. This was done by the

8 Ibn Abī Shayba, 12. See the appendix.

9 Abū Dāwūd, 166; Ibn Māja, 461; al-Nasāʾī, 1:86.

10 Muslim, 262.

Messenger of God صَلَّى ٱللَّهُ عَلَيْهِ وَسَلَّمَ, who was the shyest of people, in order to show people [that it is permitted].

How to Wipe after Urination or Defecation

[After defecation] he should use three stones to wipe [the anus clean]. If it is clean, that suffices, but if not, then a fourth, and even if it is clean, a fifth, for while cleanliness is obligatory (*wājib*), doing things an odd number of times is preferred (*mustaḥabb*), even as the Prophet صَلَّى ٱللَّهُ عَلَيْهِ وَسَلَّمَ said, "He who uses stones [for cleansing] should use an odd number."[11]

He [should] take the stone in his left hand, place it just anterior to the anus, and then pass it with a wiping motion upward over the anus. Then he [should] take the second stone and pass it with a wiping motion in the opposite direction. Then he [should] take the third stone and wipe the anal opening in a circular motion. If this last action is difficult, then wiping again from below or above the anus is sufficient. Then, taking a large stone with his right hand and his member with his left, he [should] wipe his member dry [of urine] upon the stone three times, moving it with the left hand, either to three different places on the same large stone or on three different stones, or on three places on a wall until no more moisture is seen in the spot where it is wiped, and if this can be done with two wipings, he should add a third. This is in the event that one does not wish to use more stones. If a fourth is used, however, then it is preferred to add a fifth for the sake of the odd number. Then he should take himself from that place to another place in order to cleanse with water, pouring with his right hand on the places from which urine or excrement leaves the body, and washing with [his] left hand until there are no traces of it remaining to the touch, but without searching inside [the anus], for this gives rises to whisperings of doubt. He should know that whatever does not come into contact with [the poured] water is considered internal and not subject to the rules governing impurity. What is external is defined as that

11 Muslim, 237; al-Bukhārī, 161.

which is removed by contact with water [being poured] upon it. Whisperings of doubt about this have no meaning.

Upon completing this cleansing, let him say: "O God, purify my heart from hypocrisy and guard my private parts from sin."[12]

[Then] he should rub his hand on a wall or on the earth to remove any smell left on it. To do this cleansing with both stones and water is preferred, based on what the Prophet ﷺ said to the people of Qubāʾ concerning God's words, *Within it are men who love to purify themselves and God loves those who purify themselves* [9:108]: "What is that purification which God has praised you for?" They answered, "It is that we use both water and stones."[13]

How to Perform the Lesser Ablution (*wuḍūʾ*)

After having completed the wiping and cleansing [after defecation or urination], a person should undertake the lesser ablution, for the Messenger of God ﷺ was never seen leaving [the place of] defecation without then going to perform the lesser ablution.[14]

Let him begin with the tooth stick (*siwāk*), for the Messenger of God ﷺ said, "Verily, your mouths are pathways of the Qurʾān, so sweeten them with the tooth stick."[15] Thus, in using the tooth stick, a person's intention should be to purify his mouth for the recitation of Sūrat al-Fātiḥa[16] and the mention of God most high in prayer.

He also said ﷺ, "The prayer offered after using the tooth stick is better than seventy-five prayers without."[17]

12 Abū Ṭālib al-Makkī, *Qūt al-qulūb*, 2:92. See the appendix.

13 According to al-Bazzār, the wording is "We follow [the use of stones] with water." Al-Bazzar, quoted in al-Haythamī, *Majmaʿ al-zawāʾid*, 1:217.

14 Ibn Māja, 354.

15 Ibn Māja, 291; al-Bazzār, 603.

16 The seven-verse opening chapter of the Qurʾān; its recitation is an obligatory part of each cycle (*rakaʿa*) of the prayer.

17 Ibn Ḥanbal, 6:272.

And, "If it were not for the fact that I would burden my community, I would have enjoined upon them the use of the tooth stick for every prayer."[18]

And also: "Why do I see you coming to me with yellow teeth? Use the tooth stick!"[19]

And he used to clean his teeth with it at night a number of times.[20]

According to Ibn ʿAbbās رَضِيَ ٱللَّهُ عَنْهُمَا: "The Prophet صَلَّى ٱللَّهُ عَلَيْهِ وَسَلَّمَ told us to use the tooth stick so much that we thought there would be a revelation to him concerning it."[21]

And he would say صَلَّى ٱللَّهُ عَلَيْهِ وَسَلَّمَ, "Use the tooth stick. It cleans your mouth and pleases your Lord."[22]

And ʿAlī b. Abī Ṭālib said (may God ennoble his face): "Using the tooth stick increases your memory and removes phlegm."

[Thus], the Companions of the Prophet صَلَّى ٱللَّهُ عَلَيْهِ وَسَلَّمَ would carry their tooth sticks behind their ears.[23]

The way to brush the teeth is with a piece of wood from the Arāk tree[24] or another [thin] branch of a tree that has woody fibers and removes the yellow from teeth. He should brush both laterally and up and down, but if not both, then at least laterally.

It is preferable to use the tooth stick for every prayer and at every ablution whether it is followed by the prayer or not, and for the bad breath that arises from sleep or from abstaining from food, or from eating something that has an unpleasant odor.

After using the tooth stick, let him sit facing the *qibla* for the lesser ablution. He should begin by pronouncing the formula, "In the name of God, the Merciful and Compassionate," for the Prophet صَلَّى ٱللَّهُ عَلَيْهِ وَسَلَّمَ said, "He who does not mention the name of God has no ablution,"[25] which is to say, no complete ablution.

---

18 Al-Bukhārī, 887; Muslim, 252.

19 Ibn Ḥanbal, 1:214.

20 Muslim, 763.

21 Ibn Ḥanbal, 1:339.

22 Al-Bukhārī, without an *isnād*; Ibn Ḥibbān, 1070.

23 Ibn Abī Shayba, 1805.

24 *Salvadora persica*, a short evergreen tree indigenous to the sandy regions of the Middle East and Africa.

25 Abū Dāwūd, 101; al-Tirmidhī, 25; Ibn Māja, 399. The exact wording is, "He who does not remember God has no ablution."

He should also say at this time, "I seek refuge in You from insinuations of devils and I seek refuge in You, Lord, from them being present [with me]."[26]

He should wash his hands thrice before putting them into the water container and then say, "O God, I ask of You ease and blessing and I seek refuge in You from misfortune and perdition." He should then formulate the intention either to remove impurity or to allow the prayer, and he should try to keep this intention in mind until washing the face, and if he forgets it when washing the face, the ablution is not acceptable.

Then he should take a handful of water into his mouth with his right hand and rinse his mouth three times, gargling with it so that it reaches all the way back to the larynx, except if he is fasting, in which case he [should rinse the mouth only] lightly.

Here he should say, "O God, help me in the recitation of Your book and in the abundant remembrance of You."

Then he should take a handful of water to his nose and breathe it up into his nostrils, cleaning the cartilage therein, and blowing it out, and repeat this three times. Upon taking the water into his nose, let him say, "O God, let me smell the fragrance of heaven [and] You are pleased with me," and upon blowing it back out [he should say], "O God, I seek refuge in You from the odors of the fire and the evil abode." For inhaling is contact while exhaling is removal.

Then he should take a handful of water for his face and wash its length from where the flatness of his forehead begins to the limit of where his chin protrudes [from his neck] and its width from ear to ear. The two temples at the sides of the forehead are not considered part of the face but rather part of the head. Water should also reach the place where women often trim their hair at the sides of the face, the area delineated if a piece of string were stretched from the top of the ear to the corner of the temple. Water should also reach [the skin] of the four places where facial hair grows: the eyebrows, the mustache, the eyelashes, and the sideburns, for the hair [in all these

---

26 The formula of seeking refuge appears in many supplications attributed to the Prophet. It and the other supplications in this chapter are quoted from Abū Ṭālib al-Makkī, *Qūt al-qulūb*, 2:92.

places] is generally light. Sideburns (*ʿidhārān*) mean what [extends] parallel [from] the ears to where the beard begins.

Water must reach any facial skin under a light beard but not a thick one; this rule also applies to the tuft of hair that grows from beneath the lower lip to the chin (*ʿanfaqa*).

This [washing of the face] should be done three times, [by] pouring water on the surface of a beard that grows down and using his forefinger to clean around the eye sockets from any secretions and kohl that have gathered there, for it has been related that the Prophet ﷺ did this,[27] and while cleaning around the eyes, he should hope to rid himself of their transgressions. In fact, he should hope this while washing any part of his body. And he should say, "O God, illuminate my face with Your light on the day when the faces of Your friends are illuminated, and do not darken my face with Your darkness on the day when the faces of Your foes are darkened." If he has a thick beard, it is preferred (*mustaḥabb*) that he run his [wet] fingers through it when washing his face.

Then he should wash his hands [and forearms] to the elbows three times. [If he is wearing a ring] he should move it.[28] He should extend the traces of the ablution to wash above the elbows for, as a narration affirms, the faithful will be gathered on the day of resurrection and the places they washed in the ablution [will be] illuminated. Thus, the Prophet ﷺ said, "Whoever can, should try to extend the places washed [in the ablution],"[29] and "A beautiful light (*ḥilya*) will reach the places the ablution reached."[30]

He should begin [by washing] the right hand and say, "O God, give me my book in my right hand and reckon me with an easy reckoning." Upon washing the left hand, he should say, "O God, I seek refuge in You from Your giving me my book in my left hand or behind my back."[31]

---

27 Ibn Ḥanbal, 5:258.

28 This is necessary if the ring does not allow water to reach the skin beneath it.

29 Al-Bukhārī, 136; Muslim, 246.

30 Muslim, 250. The word *ḥilya* literally means ornament. Al-Zabīdī, however, mentions that this has been explained as "a light that God will cause to shine forth from the foreheads and feet of the faithful." Al-Zabīdī, *Itḥāf*, 2:361.

31 Abū Ṭālib al-Makkī, *Qūt al-qulūb*, 2:92. Being given the book of one's deeds in the right hand is referred to in Q. 17:71, 69:19, 84:07; in the left hand in 69:25; and

Then he should wipe his head completely by wetting both hands and joining their fingertips, and then, starting at the hairline above his forehead, pass them all the way [over his head] to the nape of his neck, and from their back to the front. This is one wiping of the head, and he should do this [wiping] three times, saying as he does, "O God, cover me with Your mercy, send down upon me Your blessings, and shade me in the shade of Your throne on the day when there is no shade except Your shade."[32]

He should then wipe his ears, outside and in, with fresh water, first [he should] insert his index fingers into their openings and run his thumbs behind them in an upward arching motion, and then [he should] cover his ears completely with his hands. [This wiping] should be done three times while saying, "O God, make me among *who listen to speech and follow the best of it.* God, let me hear the one who will call [the faithful] to heaven while I am among the righteous."[33]

Then, wetting his hands anew, he should wipe the back of his neck, following the saying of the Prophet صَلَّىٱللَّهُعَلَيْهِوَسَلَّمَ, "Wiping the neck [in ablution] is safety from the shackle on the day of resurrection."[34] He should also say, "O God, free me from the fire! I seek refuge in You from chains and shackles."

He should then wash his right foot three times, washing between his toes with his left hand, beginning with the little toe of the right foot and finishing with the little toe of the left foot. [As he washes the right foot], let him say. "O God, set my feet firmly upon the straight path on the day when feet slip into fire," and as he washes the left, let him say, "I seek refuge in You from my feet slipping on

---

behind the back in 84:10.

32 Abū Ṭālib al-Makkī, *Qūt al-qulūb*, 2:92. The supplication refers to the well-known *ḥadīth*, "There are seven whom God will shade in the shade of His throne on the day when there is no shade except His shade" (al-Bukhārī, 517; Muslim, 1031).

33 Abū Ṭālib al-Makkī, *Qūt al-qulūb*, 2:92. The supplication refers to Q. 39:18: *Who listen to speech and follow the best of it. Those are the ones God has guided, and those are people of understanding.*

34 Al-Zabīdī affirms that while wiping the back of the neck is *sunna* according to the Shāfiʿī school, this saying was probably by the one of the early believers. Al-Zabīdī, *Itḥāf*, 2:365.

the traverse (*ṣirāṭ*) on the day when the feet of hypocrites will slip."[35] He should bring the water halfway up his calves.[36]

When he has finished, he should raise his head toward the sky and say,

> I bear witness that there is no god but God, alone, without partners, and I bear witness that Muḥammad is His servant and Messenger! Glory be to You, O God, and praise! There is no god but You. I have committed evil and wronged my own soul. I seek forgiveness from You, O God, and turn to You in repentance, so forgive me and accept my repentance. You are truly the Forgiving and Compassionate! O God, make me among those who turn to You in repentance and make me among those who purify themselves, and make me among Your righteous servants, and make me Your patient and grateful servant, and make me someone who invokes [You] in abundance and glorifies You morning and night.[37]

It has been said that if someone makes this supplication at the end of the lesser ablution, a seal is set upon his ablution, and it is raised up for him [and placed] beneath the throne, and continues to glorify and sanctify God most high, and the recompense of all of it is written for him on the day of resurrection.[38]

There are certain things that are disapproved of in the lesser ablution. One of them is to wash [any part of the body] more than three times. One who does so transgresses the limit, and wasting water is also disapproved of. The Prophet صَلَّى ٱللَّهُ عَلَيْهِ وَسَلَّمَ made the ablution washing each part thrice and said, "Someone who washes more than this exceeds the limit and is at fault."[39] He also said, "There will be members of this community who will go to excesses in supplication and purification."[40]

---

35 See the description of the traverse, in *Al-Ghazālī: The Remembrance of Death and the Afterlife*, translated T. J. Winter, 205.

36 Extending the washing of the forearms beyond the elbows and the washing of the feet up the calves is a recommended practice, and is not obligatory.

37 This is quoted from Abū Ṭālib al-Makkī, *Qūt al-qulūb*, 2:92.

38 Abū Ṭālib al-Makkī, *Qūt al-qulūb*, 2:92.

39 Abū Dāwūd, 135; al-Nasāʾī, 1:88.

40 Abū Dāwūd, 96; Ibn Māja, 3864.

It has been said that a man's love [of using a lot of water in the ablution] arises from the weakness of his knowledge. And Ibrāhīm b. Adham said, "The first place where whisperings arise is about purification." And Ḥasan said, "There is a devil called al-Walahān who laughs at people in their ablution."[41]

Shaking water off the hands [following the ablution], talking during it, or splashing water on the face is also disapproved of.

There are folk who disapprove of drying with a towel [during or after] and say, "The ablution will be weighed [in the scale of good actions]." Saᶜīd b. al-Musayyab and al-Zuhrī said this,[42] but it was related by Muᶜadh رَضِيَ ٱللَّهُ عَنْهُ that the Prophet صَلَّى ٱللَّهُ عَلَيْهِ وَسَلَّمَ wiped his face with part of his garment[43] and ᶜĀʾisha رَضِيَ ٱللَّهُ عَنْهَا related that he possessed a towel, but this narration is questionable.[44]

Making the ablution from a vessel made of brass[45] or using water that has been sitting in the sun is also disapproved of, the latter because of health [concerns]. The disapproval of using a brass vessel comes from what was reported from Ibn ᶜUmar and Abū Hurayra رَحِمَهُمَا ٱللَّهُ. Someone said, "I brought water to Shuᶜaba [Abū Bisṭām son of al-Ḥujāj al-ᶜAtakī, the Commander of the Faithful] in a brass vessel but he refused to make the ablution from it. This was also reported by Ibn ᶜUmar رَضِيَ ٱللَّهُ عَنْهُمَا.[46]

---

41 Al-Bayhaqī, *al-Sunan al-kubrā*, 1:197. This is also related as a *ḥadīth* in al-Tirmidhī, 57, and in Ibn Māja, 421.

42 Al-Tirmidhī, 54.

43 Al-Tirmidhī, 54; Abū Dāwūd, 245.

44 Al-Tirmidhī, 53, points to a weakness in the chain of transmission. In his commentary on Muslim, al-Nawawī says, concerning whether it is better not to use a towel after the ablution: "The third view is that it is *mubāḥ* (allowed)—to do it or not to do it are equal—and this is the view we choose, since to either prohibit it or recommend it would require clear textual proof." Al-Nawawī, *Sharḥ Ṣaḥīḥ Muslim*, 3:232.

45 "When the servant intends to make the ablution, devils gather and begin their whispering, but when he mentions the name of God, they flee and angels draw near. If the ablution is made from a vessel of copper or brass, however, angels will not approach." Abū Ṭālib al-Makkī, *Qūt al-qulūb*, 2:93.

46 This is based on a *ḥadīth* quoted in *Qūt al-qulūb* that mentions vessels of copper and brass, but then refers to a narration from Zaynab, the daughter of Jaḥsh, who said that the Prophet صَلَّى ٱللَّهُ عَلَيْهِ وَسَلَّمَ made the ablution in a *mikhḍab*, which is a large copper vessel used for washing clothes.

When a person completes the ablution, and is about to offer the prayer, he should bring to mind his outward purity, which is what people see, and so [he] should be shy [about] having intimate discourse with God most high without having purified his heart, which is what the Lord sees.

He should know with certainty that the purification of the heart comes through repentance, ridding the soul of its vices, and reforming it with virtue. [He should know, too,] that a person who stops at outward purification alone is like someone who wants to invite a king to his home, then busies himself with decorating its front door while leaving the inside full of rubbish and debris. What anger and perdition such a man as this invites upon his soul! And God most high knows best.

The Meritorious Qualities of the Lesser Ablution

The Messenger of God ﷺ said, "Whoever makes the ablution and does it well, then offers a prayer with two bowings (*rakʿatayn*) undistracted by mundane thoughts will emerge from his sins [as clean] as on the day his mother bore him," or in another version, "and is not subject to neglect is forgiven all his past sins."[47]

He also said ﷺ, "Shall I not inform you of that by which God expiates sins and raises [one's place with God] in degree? The ablution made with care in difficult conditions,[48] the steps that are taken [while walking to] mosques, and awaiting the prayer after the prayer—there is your citadel!"—and this last phrase he repeated three times.[49]

The Prophet ﷺ made the ablution once and then once again and said, "This is an ablution. Without it God does not accept the prayer." And he made the ablution twice and then twice again

47 Al-Bukhārī, 160; Muslim, 226.

48 Meaning, for example, using cold water in the winter.

49 Muslim, 251; al-Bayhaqī, *Shuʿab al-īmān*, 2483. The Arabic term translated here as "citadel" is *ribāṭ*, derived from the root r-b-ṭ, "to tie." It may be understood as a combination of spiritual retreat and military fortress for the defense of the frontier.

and said, "If someone makes the ablution twice, then twice again, God will reward him twofold." Then he made the ablution three times, then three times again and said, "This is my ablution, and the ablution of the prophets before me, and the ablution of God's intimate friend Abraham, upon him be peace!"[50]

And he said صَلَّى ٱللَّٰهُ عَلَيْهِ وَسَلَّمَ, "For the one who remembers God while performing the ablution, God purifies his entire body, while for the one who does not remember God, God purifies only those parts touched by water."[51]

And he said صَلَّى ٱللَّٰهُ عَلَيْهِ وَسَلَّمَ, "For the one who makes the ablution even while in the state of purity, God will write that he accomplished ten good deeds."[52]

And he said صَلَّى ٱللَّٰهُ عَلَيْهِ وَسَلَّمَ, "The ablution upon the ablution is light upon light."[53] All this is encouragement to renew the ablution.

And he said,

> When a Muslim servant [of God] makes the ablution and rinses his mouth, sins depart from his mouth; when he washes his nostrils, they depart from his nose; when he washes his face, they depart from his face and even from under his eyelids; when he washes his hands, they depart from his hands and even from under his fingernails; when he wipes his head, they depart from his head and even from under his ears; and when he washes his feet, they depart from his feet and even from under his toenails. Then his going to the mosque and offering the prayer are supererogatory worship![54]

It is also related that someone who remains in [a state of] purity is like someone who is fasting.[55] And he said, صَلَّى ٱللَّٰهُ عَلَيْهِ وَسَلَّمَ

50 Ibn Māja, 420; al-Ṭabarānī, *al-Muʿjam al-awsaṭ*, 6288.

51 Al-Dāraquṭnī, 1:74

52 Abū Dāwūd, 62; al-Tirmidhī, 59; Ibn Māja, 512.

53 Al-Mundharī mentions this saying in *al-Targhīb wa-l-tarhīb* with the comment, "I do not have any source that this is a *ḥadīth* of the Prophet صَلَّى ٱللَّٰهُ عَلَيْهِ وَسَلَّمَ but it may be a saying of one of the early Muslims" (1:123).

54 Al-Nasāʾī, 1:74; Mālik, 1:31; Ibn Māja, 282.

55 Al-Daylamī, 3981, where the exact wording is, "One who sleeps with the ablution is like one who stands [in prayer] fasting."

> When someone makes the ablution and does so well, then lifts his gaze toward the sky and says, "I bear witness that there is no god but God, alone, without partner, and I bear witness that Muḥammad is His servant and Messenger," the eight gates of heaven are opened to him and he enters from whichever of them he wishes.[56]

And ʿUmar رَضِيَ اللَّهُ عَنْهُ said, "The ablution done well drives Satan away from you."

And Mujāhid said, "Whoever is able to go to bed in a state of purity, remembering God, and seeking forgiveness, let him do so, for souls will be resurrected in the condition in which they were taken."[57]

How to Perform the Greater Ablution

A person should place the vessel of water on his right and then say, "*Bismillāh al-raḥmān al-raḥīm*" [In the name of God, the Merciful, the Compassionate]. Then he should wash his hands three times and wash [his] private parts in the manner I have described to you, and remove from [his] body any impurities there might be. Then he should complete the lesser ablution as if for prayer, as previously described, except for washing the feet, which should be left for later, since to wash them and then place them on the ground is a waste of water.

Then he should pour water on his head three times, then on the right side of his body three times, the left side of his body three times, and on his head three times. Then he should scrub his body front and back, and run his fingers into the hair of his head and beard, making sure that water reaches the skin beneath, whether the hair is thick or thin.

---

56 Muslim, 234, and Abū Dāwūd, 169, without the words "then lifts his gaze toward the sky."

57 Ibn Abī Shayba, 1272. A version of this *ḥadīth* has the wording, "There is no Muslim who goes to sleep in a state of purity, remembering God, then arises from the night and asks for the goodness in this world and the next except that God gives that to him."

A woman is not required to undo her braids unless she knows that water will not penetrate the hair [to reach the skin beneath].

[When washing], he should be sure to include the creases and folds of the body but take care not to touch the penis while doing this, for that necessitates repeating the ablution. [Otherwise], if he makes the lesser ablution before the greater ablution, he need not repeat it after the greater ablution.[58]

These, then, are the basic elements of the lesser and greater ablutions. We have mentioned about them only what it is indispensable for one traveling the path of the hereafter to know and do. For any questions beyond this relating to particular circumstances, one should refer to the books of jurisprudence (*fiqh*).

The absolutely essential elements (*wājib*) in all that we have mentioned concerning the greater ablution are two things: to have intention and to wash the entire body.

The obligatory elements (*furūḍ*) of the ablution are (1) intention, (2) washing the face, (3) washing the hands to the elbows, (4) scrubbing [with the hands] all that can be called the head, (5) washing the feet up to the ankles, and (6) following the proper order of actions.

It is not essential to make the greater ablution without interruption.

The greater ablution becomes obligatory [after] four things: the ejaculation of semen, the union of penis and vagina; menstruation; and [after the end of] post-partum bleeding.

For other reasons, the greater ablution is a *sunna* action. Examples of these would be [to perform it] for the two principle feasts (*ᶜids*), for the Friday prayer, upon donning the pilgrim's garb, for the standing at ᶜArafa, for the day of Muzdalifa, for each of the three days—called *ayyām al-tashrīq*—following the day of sacrifice, and, according to one point of view, for the final circumambulation upon leaving Mecca. [The greater ablution is also *sunna*] when an unbeliever who is not in a state of impurity enters Islam, for a person who has been temporarily seized by demonic possession upon recovering from [the possession], and for one who has washed a corpse for burial. In all these situations, the greater ablution is recommended [but not obligatory].

58 That is, unless something occurs which voids the lesser ablution, and for a man, this includes touching the penis with his fingers or palm.

How to Perform the Dry Ablution (*tayammum*)

A person is excused from using water [for ablution] if (1) he cannot find it after having searched; (2) he is prevented from reaching it by the threat of wild animals or [some other] obstacle; (3) water is available but he needs it to quench his thirst or that of his companion; (4) it belongs to someone who will only sell it above its fair price; or (5) he has a wound or illness and is afraid that using water would lead to infection [of the wound] or worsening of the illness. [In any of these circumstances] he should wait for the time of the obligatory prayer and then head for a clean, high place on which there is earth that is pure, unmixed with anything else, and loosen enough to be taken up [by a breeze or current of air]. Then, with the intention of making it permissible to offer the prayer, he should strike the palms of his hands upon [the soil or dust] with fingers closed and wipe his face completely one time.

[In doing this], he is not responsible for ensuring that the dust reaches the skin under his hair, whether thick or thin, but he should try to ensure that it covers his face. This can be done by striking [the dusty surface] once, for the width of the face does not exceed the width of the palms of both hands. If he is convinced that he has wiped his entire face, that is sufficient [from the standpoint of the law].

Then he should remove his ring and pat the surface [of the dust] a second time, this time with his fingers open, and then place the fingers of his right hand, palm down, upon the fingers of his left hand, palm up, so that the fingertips of both hands are even, and then draw his left hand down from where he placed it along the outside of his forearm, to the elbow. Then, turning his left hand, he should pass it from the inside of that [same] forearm to the wrist, [completing this action by] running his left thumb along the outside of his right thumb. He should then do this same action upon the left hand [and forearm], [and end] by wiping his palms together and rubbing the fingers [of both hands] between one another.

The object of this action is to wipe [the hands and arms] with a single patting [of the dust or sand], but if that is difficult for a person, then there is no harm in patting it a second time or more.

If he [then] offers the obligatory prayer with this [dry ablution], he may also follow that with whatever number of supererogatory prayers he wishes, but if he is combining obligatory prayers,[59] then he should repeat the dry ablution for the second prayer. In this same manner, the ablution without water must be done [anew] for each of the obligatory prayers. And God knows best.

59 Which may be done when traveling.

3

Cleaning What Adds to the Body Externally, of Which There Are Two Basic Kinds: The External and What Grows from the Body; and the External Consisting of Forms of Dirt and Secretions, of Which There Are Eight

FIRST, dirt and lice which collect in the hair. In respect to this, it is recommended [that one] groom the hair by washing, combing, and using a pomade,[1] all of which remove shagginess.

The Prophet صَلَّىٱللَّهُعَلَيْهِوَسَلَّمَ used to comb and [apply] pomade [to] his hair from time to time and enjoined this upon others, saying, "From time to time use a pomade."[2]

He also said صَلَّىٱللَّهُعَلَيْهِوَسَلَّمَ, "Whoever has even a single hair, let him treat it with respect!"[3] that is, by protecting it from dirt and filth.

Once a man with disheveled hair and a shaggy beard entered his presence and he said, "Does that man have no pomade to settle down his hair?" Then he said, "One of you has come in here looking like a devil!"[4]

---

1 A pamode is any oil-based product used for keeping hair in place, similar to styling gel.

2 This is reported in al-ʿAskārī, 360, and al-Ḥākim, 3504, with the wording, "Eat olive oil and use it as pomade for it comes from a blessed tree."

3 Abū Dāwūd, 4165, and elsewhere, with the wording, "Whoever has hair, let him treat it with respect."

4 Abū Dāwūd, 4062; Mālik, 2:949.

Second, dirt which accumulates in the folds of the ears. This is removed externally by the wiping [of the ablution], but [the wax] which accumulates inside the ear should be cleansed away gently upon leaving the bath, for too much of this may harm the hearing.

Third, mucus that gathers in the nostrils and clings to their inside surface, removed by inhaling and blowing out water [as in the ablution].

Fourth, the discoloration on the teeth and the edge of the tongue, removed by the tooth stick and by rinsing the mouth [in ablution] as we have mentioned.

Fifth, the dirt and lice that might collect in the beard if not groomed. It is recommended that this be removed by washing and combing. According to a well-known narration, the Prophet ﷺ was never without a comb, a hair scrubber, and mirror, whether on a journey or at home.[5] Such is an Arab custom.

According to a rare narration, the Prophet ﷺ used to comb his beard twice a day[6] and he had a thick beard, as did Abū Bakr.[7] ʿUthmān's beard, on the other hand, was long and thin, and ʿAlī's was wide, filling the space between his shoulders.

In an even rarer *ḥadīth*, ʿĀʾisha رَضِيَ ٱللَّهُ عَنْهَا is reported to have said, "A group of people gathered at the door of God's Messenger and [as he was] going out to meet them, I saw him look into [his reflection in the surface of the water in] a standing water vessel to arrange his hair and beard. I said to him, 'This is something you do, O Messenger of God?' He answered, 'Yes. God loves for His servant to show beauty to his brethren when he goes out to meet them.'"[8]

An ignorant person might suppose that this relates to a desire to appear handsome in the eyes of people, and [might] measure [this action] by the standard of those other [than God's Messenger ﷺ], which is like comparing angels to blacksmiths! How absurd! In fact, the Messenger of God ﷺ was

5 Al-Ṭabarānī, *al-Muʿjam al-awsāṭ*, 5238, with the wording, "There were five things the Prophet ﷺ was never without, whether on a journey or at home: a mirror, a kohl applier, a comb, a hair scrubber, and a tooth stick."

6 Al-Tirmidhī, *al-Shamāʾīl al-Muḥammadiyya*, 39.

7 Al-Nasāʾī, 8:183.

8 Al-Zabīdī adds, by way of explanation: "This is in order that he might show them a reflection of God's beauty." Al-Zabīdī, *Itḥāf*, 2:296.

commanded to call people [to God]. It was his responsibility to make every effort to gain respect in their hearts so as not to be taken lightly and to beautify his form in their eyes so that they would not belittle him and be turned away from him because of it. In fact, this was an excuse the hypocrites claimed in their rejection.

Such should be the purpose of every learned person who calls people to God almighty. There should be nothing in his outward appearance that would drive people away from him.

The determining factor in such matters is intention. In themselves, [methods of grooming] are actions that acquire particular qualities from the purpose [behind them]. To beautify one's appearance for the purpose [mentioned in the narration] is beloved. To leave the beard unkempt so as to appear ascetic and detached from oneself is something to be avoided, while to leave it thus because one is occupied with something more important is beloved.

These are inward conditions that exist between the servant and God عَزَّوَجَلَّ. One with discernment will not be deluded in any case.

Yet how many an ignorant man affects such things for the eyes of people, deceiving both himself and others, while pretending that his intention is good. Thus, do you see a group of the learned wearing costly and impressive garments, claiming that their purpose is to refute heretical innovators and opponents and thereby draw closer to God.

This is something that will be revealed on *the day when secrets will be put on trial* [86:9], [*the day*] *when the contents of the graves are scattered and that within the breasts is obtained* [100:9–10]. Then will true gold be distinguished from fool's gold, and we seek refuge in God from shame on the day of the greatest exposition.

Sixth, the dirt [which accumulates] on the knuckles, that is, the joints the fingers. The Arabs did not use to wash these much because they did not wash their hands after a meal. Consequently, dirt would collect there and the Messenger of God صَلَّىٱللَّهُعَلَيۡهِوَسَلَّمَ ordered that they wash them.[9]

Seventh, cleaning the fingertips, including the nails. The Messenger of God commanded the Arabs to clean their nails since

9 Al-Ḥakīm al-Tirmidhī, *Nawādir al-uṣūl*, 45, and also in the *ḥadīth* to follow.

scissors were not always available and dirt would therefore collect there. He ordered them to trim the nails, remove the hair of the armpits, and shave the pubic hair once every forty days,[10] but [he] ordered that the nails be cleaned [regularly].[11]

There is a narration that the Prophet صَلَّى ٱللَّٰهُ عَلَيْهِ وَسَلَّمَ was awaiting a revelation to come to him but it did not. Then Gabriel عَلَيْهِ ٱلسَّلَامُ came down to him and said, "How can we bring it down to you when you do not wash your knuckles, or clean your fingertips, or clean the discoloration from your teeth? Command your people to do this!"[12]

The dirt under the nails is called *uff* while that in the ears is called *tuff*. The words of almighty God, *Do not say to* [*your parents*] *'uff'* [17:23]thus means "Do not fault them for the dirt beneath their nails." It is also said to mean, "Do not find them offensive as you find offensive the dirt beneath your nails."

Eighth is the dirt that collects on the whole body because of sweat or dust from the road, all of which can be removed in the bathhouse (*ḥammām*).

Concerning the Bathhouse

[Here it should be mentioned that] there is no harm in going into a bathhouse. The Companions of the Prophet صَلَّى ٱللَّٰهُ عَلَيْهِ وَسَلَّمَ did so in Damascus.

In fact, one of them said, "What an excellent place the bathhouse is! It cleans the body and reminds us of hell!" This was reported as having been said by Abū l-Dardāʾ and Abū Ayyūb al-Anṣārī رَضِيَ ٱللَّٰهُ عَنْهُ.[13] Someone else, however, said, "What an evil place the bathhouse is! It uncovers people's nakedness and takes away their modesty!"[14]

10 Muslim, 258.

11 In al-Ṭabarānī, *Muʿjam al-kabīr*, 22:147, there is a narration from Wābiṣa b. Maʿbad, which states, "I asked the Messenger of God صَلَّى ٱللَّٰهُ عَلَيْهِ وَسَلَّمَ about everything, even about dirt under the fingernails, and he said to me, 'Leave whatever causes you doubts for that which does not cause you doubts.'"

12 Ibn Abī Shayba, 1816.

13 Ibn Abī Shayba, 1173, 1176, 1179, and al-Bayhaqī, 7:309.

14 Ibn Abī Shayba, 1172; al-Bayhaqī, 7:309. Abū Ṭālib al-Makkī also cites this saying in *Qūt al-qulūb*, 2:260, with the comment, "The views of the Companions varied

The latter speaks of its dangers while the former speaks of its benefits, and there is nothing wrong with seeking its benefits if one guards against its danger.

There are, thus, certain rules—both *sunna* and obligatory—that should be observed upon entering the bathhouse.

In respect to what is obligatory, there are two rules concerning one's own nakedness and two concerning the nakedness of others.

As for the two concerning one's own nakedness, they are to keep the area of one's body considered private out of the view of, or contact with, someone else. Thus, he attends to this area [himself] and cleans it with his own hand and does not allow the bath attendant[15] to touch the thigh or below the navel. There is a difference of opinion about [whether it is] permissible [for the scrubber] to scrub all but the pubic area in order to remove dirt, but the most fitting practice is to respect its prohibition, since to touch this area entails looking at it, and looking at it is prohibited. This should apply to the rest of one's nakedness as well, by which is meant the thighs.

In respect to the two obligations concerning the nakedness of others, the first [obligation] is that he should lower his gaze from viewing it, and the second is that he should tell the other who uncovers his [own] nakedness [in his presence] that [what he is doing] is prohibited, for it is obligatory to speak out against wrong. It is his duty to mention this but not to enforce its acceptance, and he is not excused from this duty except out of fear that he will be struck, verbally abused, or become the object of some other kind of retribution which itself is forbidden. In other words, it is not a duty for him to prohibit something which is unlawful if it is going to result in something else which is unlawful. This does not mean, however, that one has an excuse to say, "I know [my saying this] will not benefit him and I know he will not follow it." For no heart is beyond being affected by disapproval and taking stock if its sins are pointed out.

For reasons such as these, it has become the prevailing view these days [simply] to avoid going into bathhouses. They are never

---

concerning entering the bathhouse and in each view there is a model and a form of guidance [to be followed]."

15 *Dallāk*, literally, someone who scrubs people's bodies for a living.

free of exposed nakedness, especially if we are speaking of the area from the navel to the pubes. People do not even consider this nakedness even though [Islamic] law does and makes it, as it were, a limit not to be trespassed.

It has even been recommended [to pay] for the bathhouse to be emptied of people. Bishr b. al-Ḥārīth said, "I would not blame a man for spending his last dirham to have the bathhouse emptied," and Ibn ʿUmar رَضِيَ ٱللَّهُ عَنْهُمَا was seen in the bathhouse facing the wall with a cloth over his eyes.[16] Someone even said, "There is no harm in entering the bathhouse as long as you have two clothes to wear: one around your loins to cover your nakedness and one worn on your head to protect your eyes."[17]

On the *Sunna* Practices [Relating to the Bathhouse], These Number Ten

First is intention. This means that someone should not enter the bathhouse for some mundane end, nor to satisfy an egoistic whim, but rather for the sake of the cleanliness desired to be beautiful for prayer.

[Second], then he should pay the bath attendant his fee before entering the bath. Since both the service he will receive and the amount that the attendant expects are unknown, to pay the fee in advance eliminates one of these and puts him at ease.[18]

[Third], then, he should step into the bathhouse itself with his left foot and say, "In the name of God, Merciful and Compassionate. I seek refuge in God from abomination, impurity, corruption, and the corrupter, Satan the accursed."[19]

[Fourth], then, he should enter [the bathhouse] at a time when it is deserted or else pay to have it emptied of other people. Even if there was no one in the bath except people of religion who cover

16 Abū Ṭālib al-Makkī, *Qūt al-qulūb*, 2:260.

17 Abū Ṭālib al-Makkī, *Qūt al-qulūb*, 2:261.

18 That is, for the attendant. The bather, however, does not know the kind of service he will receive. Al-Zabīdī, *Itḥāf*, 2:402.

19 See the appendix.

their nakedness, still seeing uncovered bodies lacks modesty and to some extent it calls to mind seeing [people's] nakedness. Moreover, when people move around in the bathhouse, it is inevitable that the folds of their loin cloths come open and their nakedness is unexpectedly exposed. This is why Ibn ʿUmar رَضِيَ اللهُ عَنْهُمَا covered his eyes with a cloth [as was mentioned].

[Fifth], he should wash both hands upon entering.

[Sixth], he should not hurry into the hottest room [of the bathhouse] until he sweats for a while in the first room.

[Seventh], he should not pour a great deal of water on himself. Rather, he should try to limit his use to what is actually necessary. The amount permitted depends on the situation, but if the bathhouse attendant knows he is using more than [necessary], he would be displeased, especially in the case of hot water, which has to be specially supplied and takes great effort to make ready.

[Eighth], is that the heat of the bathhouse should remind him of the heat of hell. Let him think about [what] it would be like to be imprisoned in that hot chamber for an hour and compare that to hell, for that chamber resembles hell—fire below and darkness above—and we seek refuge in God from that! Indeed, the intelligent person will not be heedless of the remembrance of the hereafter even for an instant, for that is his destination and that is his ultimate abode. In all that he sees—be it water or fire or anything else—there will be for him a teaching and a warning, for a person looks at things according to what matters most to him. If a rug merchant, a carpenter, a builder, and a weaver enter a furnished house and you could watch them, you would see the rug merchant looking at the carpeting and thinking about its value, the weaver looking at the upholstery and thinking about its weave, the carpenter looking at the ceiling and thinking about how it was constructed, and the builder looking at the walls and thinking about how straight and well-constructed they are.

So it is with the traveler on the path of the hereafter: he sees nothing of things except what will teach him and remind [him] of the hereafter. In all that he looks upon, God opens for him a way to learn from it. Thus, if he beholds something black, he is reminded of the darkness of the grave; if he sees a snake, it recalls to his mind the vipers of hell; if he beholds something ugly and repulsive, he is reminded of Munkar, Nakīr, and the guardians of hell (*al-zabāniyya*); if he hears a frightening sound, he is reminded of the sounding of the horn [that will signal the Last Day]; and likewise, if he sees something beautiful, he remembers the bliss of heaven, and if he hears a word of rejection or acceptance in the marketplace or at home, it reminds him that in the end, after the reckoning, all that he accomplished [in life] will be either rejected or accepted.

How much more fitting for the intelligent man that this should so prevail in his heart that nothing distracts him from it except the exigencies of the world, and if he compares the length of his stay in this world with the next [world], he will disdain the former unless he is someone whose heart has become heedless and whose spiritual insight is lost.

Other *sunna* practices: [ninth], upon entering the bath, he should not verbally greet [those inside] with the salutation of peace,[20] and if he is so greeted, he should not return the salutation. Rather, he should remain silent [even] if someone else returns [the greeting]. If he wishes, however, he may say, "May God pardon you."[21]

There is no harm in shaking hands with someone who is entering the bathhouse and saying "May God pardon you," [if you are the one who] initiates speech, but there should not be a lot of talk inside the bathhouse, nor should the Qurʾān be recited except silently. There is no harm, however, in voicing the formula of refuge (*istiʿādh*) from Satan.

Entering the bath between the two evening prayers or just before sunset is disapproved of, for that is a time when devils roam.

There is no harm if someone else scrubs him, for it has been related that before his death, Yūsuf b. Asbāṭ gave instructions that a particular person who was not one of his companions should be allowed to wash his body [for burial], saying, "He once scrubbed me in the bathhouse and I wanted to repay him with something which would please him—and I am sure this will please him."[22]

---

20 That is, the greeting "*al-salām ʿalaykum*."

21 *ʿĀfak Allāh*, meaning, "May God efface your sins and infirmities." Al-Zabīdī, *Itḥāf*, 2:404.

22 Quoted in Abū Ṭālib al-Makkī, *Qūt al-qulūb*, 2:261.

Its permissibility is proven by what one of the Companions related: "On one of his journeys, the Messenger of God ﷺ stopped at an encampment along the way and lay down on his stomach and a black slave massaged his back. I asked, 'What is it, O Messenger of God?' and he replied, 'The she-camel threw me.'"[23]

[Tenth], when a person finishes his bath, he should give thanks to God almighty for this blessing. For it has been said, "Hot water in the winter is among the blessings concerning which people will be asked,"[24] and Ibn ʿUmar رَضِيَ اللَّهُ عَنْهُمَا said, "The bathhouse is among the blessings that were innovated."[25]

All this is from the standpoint of the [revealed] law.

From the standpoint of medical science, it has been said: "A bath in the bathhouse following depilation guards against leprosy," and "Depilation once a month removes jaundice, purifies the complexion, and increases virility," and "To urinate standing up in the bathhouse in winter is more beneficial that drinking medicine," and "A short sleep in the summer following a visit to the bathhouse is like a drink of medicine," and "Washing the feet with cold water after leaving the bath is a protection from gout."

Also, drinking or pouring cold water on one's head after coming out of the bath is disapproved of.

Such are the rulings which pertain to men.

As for those pertaining to women, the Prophet ﷺ once said, "It is not permissible for a man to let his wife go to the bathhouse when there is a place with hot water in the home."[26]

It is well-known [among people] that it is forbidden for a man to enter the bathhouse without a loincloth and [it is] forbidden

---

23 Al-Ṭabarānī, *al-Muʿjam al-ṣaghīr*, 1:83.

24 This is a reference to Q. 102:8: *Then you will surely be asked that day about pleasure.* Al-Qushayrī's Qurʾān commentary on this verse mentions hot water.

25 Abū Ṭālib al-Makkī, *Qūt al-qulūb*, 2:261.

26 Al-Tirmidhī, 2801, where the wording is "Whoever believes in God and the Last Day will not enter the bathhouse without a loin cloth; and whoever believes in God and the Last Day will not permit his wife to enter the bathhouse; and whoever believes in God and the Last Day will not sit at a table where wine is being passed around."

for a woman to enter a bathhouse except [to purify herself from] post-partum bleeding or because she is ill.[27]

ʿĀʾisha رَضِيَ ٱللَّهُ عَنْهَا, in fact, entered a bathhouse because of an illness she had.[28] If a woman does so out of necessity, she should have clothing that wraps around her and covers her.

[Finally], it is disapproved for a man to give his wife the fee for the bathhouse if this is going to aid her in [something] that is disapproved.

The Second Kind of Substances [to be Removed] from the Body are What Grows from It and These Number Eight

First, the hair of the head. There is no harm in either shaving it off for the sake of cleanliness and or letting it grow if a person tends it and uses pomade. It should not, however, be left to grow in tufts—that is, shaved in places and growing in places—for this is a habit of charlatans; nor should it be made into long braids after the style of nobles, since this has become their distinctive mark and if someone is not of them, then to [wear the hair in this style] is deceptive.

Second, the mustache. The Prophet صَلَّى ٱللَّهُ عَلَيْهِ وَسَلَّمَ said, "Trim (*quṣṣū*) the mustache," and in another version, "Cut the mustache (*juzzū*)," and yet another, "Curve (*ḥuffū*) the mustache and let the beard grow."[29] Here, "curving" means to shape the mustache so that it encircles the lip, for the *ḥifāf* actually means "encircling," as in [the words of God], *And you will see the angels encircling* (*ḥāffīna*) *the throne* [39:75]. In another version of this *ḥadīth*, the verb is *uḥfū*, which means "clip it extremely short," while *ḥuffū* indicates something less extreme than that. This former verb appears in

27 Abū Dāwūd, 4011, where the wording is "The Messenger of God صَلَّى ٱللَّهُ عَلَيْهِ وَسَلَّمَ said to us, 'Verily, you will be given victories in foreign lands where you will find houses called *ḥamāmāt* (hot baths). Let no man enter there without a loin cloth, and prohibit them (*amnaʿūhā*) to women except if they are ill or [need to bathe after the cessation of] post-partum bleeding.'"

28 Abū Ṭālib al-Makkī, *Qūt al-qulūb*, 2:261.

29 Al-Bukhārī, 5892; Muslim, 259, 260.

the words of God, *If He should ask you for them and press you* (fa yuḥfikum), *you would withhold* [47:37], meaning "if God were to press you to the limit" [in giving charity].

Shaving [the mustache] off completely (*ḥalq*) is not mentioned [in the narrations], but clipping it very short (*iḥfāʾ*) is close to shaving. Concerning the Companions, it is related that one of the successors (*tābiʿīn*) saw a man whose mustache was clipped very short and said, "You remind me of the Companions of God's Messenger صَلَّى ٱللَّٰهُ عَلَيْهِ وَسَلَّمَ."

And al-Mughīra b. Shuʿba said, "The Messenger of God صَلَّى ٱللَّٰهُ عَلَيْهِ وَسَلَّمَ looked at me and saw that my mustache had grown long and said, 'Come over here and trim your mustache for me along [the straight edge of] a tooth stick!'"[30]

There is no harm in leaving the ends of the mustache to grow down, as ʿUmar رَضِيَ ٱللَّٰهُ عَنْهُ and others did, for they did not cover the mouth nor did morsels of food cling to them. The words of the Prophet صَلَّى ٱللَّٰهُ عَلَيْهِ وَسَلَّمَ, "Spare your beards,"[31] mean "let them grow full."

According to a tradition: "The Jews let their mustaches grow and cut their beards, so you should be different from them."[32] In fact, some of the learned disapprove [entirely] of shaving and consider it an innovation.[33]

Third, the hair of the armpit. It is preferred to depilate under the arms once every forty days. This is easy for anyone who gets used to doing it from the beginning [when he or she began using this method], but for the one who is used to shaving, that suffices, for depilation is painful and torturous. Its purpose is cleanliness and to avoid the collection of dirt in the hairs of the armpit, and shaving accomplishes this.

Fourth, pubic hair. It is recommended that this be removed by shaving or using a depilatory not less than once every forty days.

---

30 Abū Dāwūd, 188.

31 Al-Bukhārī, 5443; Muslim, 380.

32 Ibn Ḥanbal, 5:264, with the wording: "O Messenger of God, the people of the Book trim their beards and let their mustaches grow long." To which the Prophet صَلَّى ٱللَّٰهُ عَلَيْهِ وَسَلَّمَ replied, "Trim your mustaches and let your beards grow long, and be unlike the people of the Book."

33 By whom he means Imām Mālik (and others like him), who included shaving the beard among the harmful innovations. See Al-Ruʿaynī, *Mawāhib al-jalīl,* 1:313.

Fifth, [finger and toe] nails. It is recommended that these be kept trimmed because they are ugly when they grow long and also because dirt collects beneath them. The Messenger of God ﷺ said, "O Abū Hurayra! Trim your nails, for Satan sits upon the part of them that grows long!"[34]

Dirt under the nails, however, does not compromise the validity of the ablution because it does not prevent water from coming into contact with [with the entire hand or foot]. Leniency arises from necessity, especially in respect to [dirt under] the toenails. Concerning the dirt that gathers on the knuckles and the backs of the hands and feet, the Messenger of God ﷺ enjoined upon both the nomadic Arabs and those who dwell in settlements that [they] trim [their nails] and he rebuked them for the dirt he saw under them but did not order them to repeat the prayer [because of it]. Had he done so, there would have been another benefit in it for them: to be strict about this [aspect of cleanliness].

I have not seen a narration in any of the books about the order in which nails should be trimmed, but I have heard that the Prophet ﷺ began with his right index finger and finished with the thumb and then began the left hand trimming the little finger and ending with the left thumb.

When I thought about this, something occurred to me which indicates that it is genuine. Matters such as these are not initially unveiled except by the light of prophethood and the most that a scholar with insight can do is apply his intelligence to finding the meaning of any practice that has come to him by transmission.

Thus, what occurred to me—and all knowledge is with God, may He be glorified! —is that [first] both fingernails and toenails must be trimmed, that the hand is nobler than the foot and so should come first, and that the right hand is nobler than the left, and so should come first. Then, of the five fingers on the right hand, the index finger is noblest, since of all the fingers it is the one used to gesture when [a believer] recites the twofold testimony of faith. Following it, someone should begin with what is to its right since the [revealed] law recommends starting the ablution and other actions from the

34 Al-Daylamī, 4579.

right. If the back of the right hand were placed flat upon the ground, immediately to right of the index finger would be the thumb, while if the hand were placed palm down on the ground, immediately to the right of the index finger would be the middle finger. But if the hand were just left in its natural position, the palm would be in the direction of the ground since its [normal] movement is from right to left, which leaves the back of the hand up, and whatever is [the more] natural takes precedence. In addition, if one palm is placed against the other, the fingers form, as it were, a circular shape, which results in the order beginning with the right index finger and ending with the index finger [of the left hand]. So, for the left hand, the little finger comes first and the thumb last. Trimming, thus, ends with the thumb of the right hand.

So, I have chosen to place the palms one against the other so that the fingers become like parts in a circle, as [this is] the best way of determining the order [in which the nails should be trimmed] because it is a more natural position than placing the palm of one hand against the back of the other, or the backs of the two hands against one another.

Concerning the toes, since no narration about it has been affirmed, then I would choose to begin with the big toe of the right foot and end with the big toe of the left foot, following the order one would when washing between the toes in the ablution. What we have mentioned concerning the hands does not apply here since the toes do not have an equivalent to the index finger. The feet, instead, form a single row when placed firmly on the ground and the action moves from right [to left]. Also, unlike with the hands, it would be unnatural for them to form a circle, one sole against the other.

Such details concerning the order of actions become clear in an instant by the light of prophethood. If we were to go on at length concerning it, it would weary us and if we were to begin with the order of actions [alone], perhaps nothing would occur to us. But as soon as we recall the actions of the Prophet ﷺ and the order in which he did them, perhaps it becomes easy for us.

And do not suppose that the actions of the Prophet ﷺ—in all his movements—departed from a standard, a code, and an order. In all matters in which there is a choice, and the actor is undecided between two or more alternatives, he should not proceed with a particular one simply by chance, but rather in a meaningful way, which necessitates giving priority to one thing or another. For acting haphazardly, in whatever way is easiest, is the characteristic of animals, while governing actions according to a meaningful standard is the characteristic of God's saints.

The nearer a person's actions and thoughts are to the standard and the further they are from being haphazard and neglectful of the standard, the closer that person's spiritual degree will be to that of the saints and prophets, and the more manifest his proximity to almighty God will be, inasmuch as anyone near the Prophet ﷺ is near God: anyone near [the Prophet], who is near God, the eternally near, must be nearer [God] than someone else. We seek refuge in God from our movements and rest, [that they not be] in the hand of Satan [because of our] passions and whims.

Consider the very specific way in which the Prophet ﷺ applied kohl to his eyes. He applied it three times to the right eye and twice to the left,[35] he began with the right eye because of its nobility, and made the number of applications from one eye to the other differ, so that the total [number of] applications was an odd number. This is because, according to his saying ﷺ: "God most high is odd-numbered and loves the odd-numbered,"[36] the odd number is more excellent than the even and the actions of the servant should not be without some relationship to the attributes of God most high. Thus, even for wiping with stones after urination or defecation, the odd number is preferred. [Applications of kohl] were not limited to three, however, even though it is an odd number, because if the right eye, which is preferred, were given the greater number, that would leave only one for the left eye, which is not enough to cover both eyelids.

And if you ask, "Then why did he limit the left eye to two applications, when that is an even number?" The answer to this is that it comes from necessity, for had he given each eye an odd number of applications, then the total number would be even, the sum of two odd numbers being even, and it is recommended to observe this

35 Ibn Abī Shayba, 23953.

36 Al-Bukhārī, 6410; Muslim, 2677.

[form] as a single action for both eyes rather than separate actions for each eye, but there is another possibility, which is to apply kohl to each eye three times, following the pattern of the ablution. This has been reported in an authentic [*ḥadīth*] and therefore is preferred.[37]

If I were to try to study all the details of what the Prophet ﷺ observed, this would become much too long, so measure what you have not heard upon the scale of what you have heard.[38]

Know that no scholar will become heir to the Prophet ﷺ[39] until he looks into the totality of meanings found in the [revealed] law and there remains but one degree between him and the Prophet ﷺ, and that is the degree of prophethood, which is the degree that separates the inheritor from the one who leaves the inheritance. One who leaves an inheritance attained wealth by working toward it until it was his, while the inheritor has neither attained wealth nor earned it, but rather has had it passed on to him and, after receiving it, will pass it to someone else.

While examples such as these are simple in comparison to the profundities and mysteries [of faith], no one fully grasps them at their inception except the prophets and no one fully discovers [the meanings they contain] after having been given them by the prophets except the scholars, who are the true heirs of the prophets.

The sixth and seventh growths to be removed are what is left of the umbilical cord and foreskin. The former is removed at birth. As for purification through circumcision, it is the habit of the Jews to do this on the seventh day after the birth, but it is preferable and safer to differ from them by delaying it until the child cuts his front teeth.

The Prophet ﷺ said, "Circumcision is *sunna* for men and honorable for women."[40]

---

37 Al-Tirmidhī, 1757; Ibn Māja, 3499.

38 "Try to consider any observance of the Prophet ﷺ that are not narrated here in light of what has been narrated, and their spiritual relationship and divine order will become clear to you. Who knows this, knows it and who does not, does not." Al-Zabīdī, *Itḥāf*, 2:417.

39 He is referring to the well-known *ḥadīth*, narrated in the collection Abū Dāwūd, Ibn Māja, and others: "The scholars are the heirs of the prophets." See also Ibn Rajab al-Ḥanbalī, *The Heirs of the Prophets*, translated by Zaid Shakir.

40 Ibn Ḥanbal, 5:75; al-Bayhaqī, *al-Sunan al-kubrā*, 8:324.

But this action for women should not be excessive. The Prophet صَلَّى ٱللَّهُ عَلَيْهِ وَسَلَّمَ said to Umm ʿAṭiyya, who used to perform circumcision [on women], "O Umm ʿAṭiyya, take only a small 'whiff' (*ashimmī*) of the prepuce and do not be excessive, for it gives color to the face and is more appealing for a husband."[41] That is, it increases the moisture of the face and the blood and [is] better for her [during] intercourse.

Behold the delicacy of the Prophet's language concerning this, and behold the prophetic light shining forth from what is beneficial in the hereafter—this being the most important goal of prophethood—to what is beneficial in this life, so that even an issue such as this, which might have had harmful results had he been left unaware of it, was unveiled to him, an unlettered man.

So, glory be to the One who sent him as a mercy for all people, that by the blessing of his coming, what is beneficial in this world and beneficial in religion might be joined, may peace and God's blessings be upon him!

Eighth is the part of the beard that grows long. We have put off discussing this so that we might include mention of the *sunna* practices and the innovations that relate to it, for this is the most suitable place in which to speak of them.

People have disagreed concerning how long [one] should let the beard grow. It has been said, for example, that if a man grasps his beard and then cuts what is longer than his grasp, there is no harm, and this was done by Ibn ʿUmar and a group of the followers and approved of by al-Shaʿbī and Ibn Sīrīn.

---

41 Al-Bayhaqī, *Sunan al-kubrā*; 8:324; al-Ṭabarānī, *Muʿjam al-awsāṭ*, 2274. It is important to point out that while there is universal agreement among Muslims that it is *sunna* to remove the foreskin of the male (and for some schools of *fiqh*, obligatory), there is no agreement about removing a small part of the clitoral hood (prepuce) of the female. Today, it is most prevalent among populations following the Shāfiʿī school of jurisprudence, but even this school does not claim that this is a religious obligation for women. Second, both the *ḥadīth* quoted here are considered to have weaknesses (*ḍaʿīf*) in their narrative chains. Third, *ḥadīth* sources explain that Umm ʿAṭiyya was a *khāfiḍa* (a woman who performed this operation on women) in Medina before Islam came to that city. In this context, the words of the Prophet صَلَّى ٱللَّهُ عَلَيْهِ وَسَلَّمَ were a warning to her that although this operation was being done in Arabia at the time, it could be harmful to a woman's sexual pleasure unless it was very minimal.

Both Ḥasan and Qatāda, however, disapproved of this practice and said, "Letting it grow is preferable to us,"[42] in keeping with the Prophet's words ﷺ "Spare your beards."[43]

This matter is simple: [it is permissible to trim the beard] as long as a man does not wind up trimming and rounding the beard on the sides, for if a beard becomes excessively long, it becomes unsightly and incites the tongues of backbiters and critics to ridicule. If the intention [in trimming it is] to protect oneself from this, then there is no harm in it.

Al-Nakhaʿī said, "I am amazed by a man of sound mind with a long beard. Why does he not cut it and make it [of a] medium length, between a long and short beard, since the middle way in all things is best." Thus, has it been said, "As the beard gets longer, the mind gets smaller."[44]

42 Abū Ṭālib al-Makkī, *Qūt al-qulūb*, 2:144.

43 Al-Bukhārī, 5892; Muslim, 259, 260.

44 Abū Ṭālib al-Makkī, *Qūt al-qulūb*, 2:145.

4

Practices That Are Disapproved of Concerning the Beard

THESE are ten in number, some of which are worse than others. These are dyeing the beard black; whitening the beard with sulfur; plucking the beard; plucking only the gray hairs out of it; shortening or lengthening it [as explained below]; tending it for the sake of ostentation; leaving it disheveled for the sake of appearing ascetic; seeing its blackness as sign of youth and marveling at that, or seeing its whiteness as a sign of venerable age; and dyeing the beard either red or yellow for the sake of imitating the people of righteousness.

First, dyeing the beard black. This is prohibited based on the saying of the Prophet صَلَّىٱللَّهُعَلَيْهِوَسَلَّمَ: "The best of your youth are those who resemble your elders and the worst of your elders are those who resemble your youth."[1]

[In this *ḥadīth*], 'resembling your elders' means in their dignity, not in the whiteness of their hair. He prohibited coloring the hair black[2] and said, "Dyeing the hair black [is a mark] of the people of hell," or in another version, "of the unbelievers."[3]

During the time of ʿUmar b. al-Khaṭṭāb رَضِيَٱللَّهُعَنْهُ a man who had dyed his hair black was married. Then the blackness faded and his grayness appeared. The family of the woman took him to

1 Al-Ṭabarānī, *al-Muʿjam al-awsāṭ*, 5900.

2 Muslim, 2012.

3 Al-Ḥākim, 3:526, with the wording, "Black is the dye of the disbeliever."

ʿUmar رَضِيَ اللَّهُ عَنْهُ, who annulled the marriage and gave him a painful slap and said, "You deceived people by trying to look young and hiding your grayness from them!"[4]

It is said that the first person to dye his hair black was Pharaoh, may God curse him.[5]

According to Ibn ʿAbbās رَضِيَ اللَّهُ عَنْهُمَا, the Prophet صَلَّى اللَّهُ عَلَيْهِ وَسَلَّمَ said, "At the end of time, there will be a people who will dye their hair as black as pigeons' gullets. They will not smell the perfume of heaven."[6]

Second, dyeing the beard yellow or red. It is permissible to do this in order to conceal gray hair from the unbelievers in combat. Otherwise, if it is not with this intention, but rather for the sake of appearing to be a religious person, then it is blameworthy. The Messenger of God صَلَّى اللَّهُ عَلَيْهِ وَسَلَّمَ said, "Yellow is the color of the Muslims; red is the color of the faithful (*al-muʾminīn*)."[7]

They would use henna for the red coloring and *khulūq* and *katam*.[8] Some of the scholars dyed their beards black for battle and there is no harm in this because the intention is correct and is not related to whims or selfish desires.

Third, whitening the beard with sulfur so that [a young man] may appear older than his years, as a way of gaining respect, or having [his] testimony accepted, or his narrations believed by the masters, or as a way of setting himself above the youth, or pretending to be a person of great knowledge under the false supposition that the many years of [his] life will make him somehow superior. What folly! Old age adds nothing to someone who is ignorant except more ignorance! Knowledge is the fruit of intelligence, and intelligence is something innate and unaffected by gray hair. Indeed, if someone's inherent nature is idiocy, a longer life will only confirm his idiocy!

Moreover, there have been venerable elders who would defer to youth in their knowledge. ʿUmar b. al-Khaṭṭāb رَضِيَ اللَّهُ عَنْهُ, for example,

---

4 Quoted in Abū Ṭālib al-Makkī, *Qūt al-qulūb*, 2:144.

5 Abū Ṭālib al-Makkī, *Qūt al-qulūb*, 2:144.

6 Abū Dāwūd, 4212; al-Nasāʾī, 8:138.

7 Abū Ṭālib al-Makkī, *Qūt al-qulūb*, 2:144; al-Ḥākim, 3:526.

8 *Khuluq* is made from saffron and other substances. *Katam* is a plant in the privet family that is indigenous to Yemen. Its leaves produce a dark gray dye.

used to defer to Ibn ʿAbbās رضي الله عنهما, who was quite young, over much elder Companions and would ask him [questions] rather than them.[9]

And Ibn ʿAbbās said رضي الله عنهما: "God most high has not given any servant knowledge except as a youth. All goodness is in young people!" And then he recited God's words: *They said, "We heard a young man mention them, and* [*he*] *is called Abraham*" [21:60] and, *They were youths who believed in their Lord, and We increased them in guidance* [18:13], and *We gave him judgment* [*while yet*] *a boy* [19:12].[10]

Anas رضي الله عنه said, "When the Messenger of God صلى الله عليه وسلم was taken [by death] there were twenty gray hairs upon his head and beard."[11] And they said to him, "O Abū Ḥamza, even with his advanced age?" He replied, "God did not shame him with gray hair." They asked, "Is gray hair a shame?" And he replied, "All of you hate it!"[12]

It is also said that Yaḥyā b. Aktham was made a judge at the age of twenty-one. Once, a man who was in his court said, wishing to embarrass him because of his youth, "How old is the judge, may God help him?" To which he replied, "The same age as ʿAttāb b. Usayd when the Messenger of God صلى الله عليه وسلم appointed him as governor of Mecca and head of its courts," at which the man was speechless.[13]

And it is narrated that Mālik, may God's mercy be upon him, said, "I have read in one of the books: "Do not be fooled by a beard. The billy goat has one too!"[14]

Abū ʿAmr b. al-ʿAlāʾ said: "If you see a man who is tall, has a small head, but wears a long thick beard, you should reckon him a fool, even if he were Umayya b. ʿAbd Shams!"[15]

Ayyūb al-Sakhtayānī said: "I have met an elder who is eighty-years-old but follows a servant boy and learns from him."

---

9 As referred to in al-Bukhārī, 4294.

10 Abū Ṭālib al-Makkī, *Qūt al-qulūb*, 2:145.

11 This is mentioned in al-Bukhārī, 3574, and in Muslim, 2347.

12 Ibn Ḥanbal, 3:108.

13 Abū Ṭālib al-Makkī, *Qūt al-qulūb*, 2:145.

14 Abū Ṭālib al-Makkī, *Qūt al-qulūb*. The Mālik referred to is Mālik b. Mighwāl (d. 159/775), who figures in the chains of transmission of scores of *ḥadīth*. Al-Zabīdī, *Itḥāf*, 2:424.

15 The venerable ancestor of the Umayyad tribe. Al-Zabīdī, *Itḥāf*, 2:424.

And ʿAlī b. al-Ḥusayn said: "Someone who has acquired knowledge before you is your *imām* concerning it, even if he is younger than you."

Abū ʿAmr b. al-ʿAlāʾ was asked: "Is it good for an elder to learn from a youth?" He answered, "If ignorance has been bad for him, learning will do him good."

After Yahyā b. Muʿīn saw Aḥmad b. Ḥanbal walking behind a mule on which al-Shāfiʿī was riding, he said to him, "O Abū ʿAbdallāh, have you abandoned the teachings of the venerable Sufyān[16] and now walk beside the mule of this young man instead, to hear his [teachings]?" Aḥmad answered, "If you only knew, you would be walking on the other side! If I miss a portion of the knowledge Sufyān has to convey directly, I can get it from others, but if I miss learning something from the intellect of this young man, I will not get it directly or from anyone else."[17]

Fourth, to pluck out white hairs out of an aversion to old age. The Prophet ﷺ prohibited this practice and said, "Gray hair is the believer's light."[18] This is understood in the same sense as dyeing it black, and the reasons that it is disapproved have been mentioned above. Gray hair is a light from God and to be averse to it is to be averse to that light.

Fifth, to pluck out the beard or some portion of it for frivolity and folly. This is both disapproved of and disfiguring to a man's appearance, while plucking the hairs off the two sides of the lower lip (*fanīkayn*) is [considered] an innovation.

A man who plucked the sides of his lower lip appeared as a witness [in a judgment] before ʿUmar b. ʿAbd al-ʿAzīz and ʿUmar refused his testimony, while both ʿUmar b. al-Khaṭṭāb رَضِيَ ٱللَّهُ عَنْهُ and Ibn Abī Layla, the judge (*qāḍī*) of Medina, refused the testimony of men who plucked their beards.[19]

---

16 That is, Sufyān b. ʿUyayna al-Kūfī, d. 198/814. Al-Zabīdī, *Itḥāf*, 2:424.

17 Abū Ṭālib al-Makkī, *Qūt al-qulūb*, 2:145.

18 Abū Dāwūd, 4202, al-Tirmidhī, 2821, and Ibn Māja, 3721, with the wording, "Do not pluck out gray hair, for it is a Muslim's light. If someone turns gray in Islam, he will have good deeds written for him because of it, faults removed because of it, and be raised in degree because of it." Al-Zabīdī, *Itḥāf*, 2:425.

19 Abū Ṭālib al-Makkī, *Qūt al-qulūb*, 2:144.

As for plucking the beard in its first growth so as to keep the look of an adolescent, this is among the most disapproved of practices, for the beard is adornment for men. God, may He be glorified, has angels who swear, "By the One who beautifies the sons of Adam with beards."[20] It is part of the perfection of creation and what distinguishes men from women.

In a rare interpretation of God's words, *He increases in creation what He wills* [35:1], some have said that what is meant is the beard.

The companions of al-Aḥnaf b. Qays said, "[Were it possible], we would buy al-Aḥnaf a beard even if it cost twenty thousand!"

And Shurayḥ al-Qāḍī said, "I would have loved to have a beard, [and if one could be bought] I would pay ten thousand!"

Indeed, how could a beard be disliked when it brings to a man esteem, allows him to be seen with knowledge and dignity, elevates him in assemblies, turns faces his way, gives him precedence in a gathering, and protects him from insult, since a reviler is slow to revile one who is bearded.

It has been said that the people of heaven are beardless except for Aaron, brother of Moses (peace be upon them both), whose beard reaches his navel to mark his distinction and excellence.[21]

Sixth, to clip the beard into rows, one upon the other, for the purpose of affectation and to look attractive to women. Kaʿb said, "At the end of time there will be people who cut their beard like pigeons' tails and curl up the toes of their sandals like scythes and they will be devoid of morals."

Seventh, to increase the beard [to reach] the hair of the temples, which is actually the hair of the head, until it meets the beard and covers half the cheeks, for this is contrary to the appearance of the righteous.

Eighth [and ninth], to comb the beard for the sake of people. Bishr said, "There are two forms of idolatry connected to the beard.

---

20 Ibn ʿAsākir, 36:343. It has also been reported by Ibn Qutayba, 4:55, as something ʿĀʾisha رضي الله عنها said.

21 This presumably relates to Aaron saying to Moses: *"O son of my mother, do not seize* [*me*] *by my beard or by my head. Indeed, I feared that you would say, 'You caused division among the children of Israel, and you did not observe* [*or await*] *my word.'"* [20:94].

One is to comb it for the sake of people and the other is to leave it tangled so as to look ascetic."[22]

Tenth and eleventh, to look upon either the blackness or whiteness of a beard as something impressive. This is a fault in respect to any part of the body. In fact, it is a fault in respect to any aspect of one's character or actions as will be explained later [in this work].

This is all that we intended to mention concerning the varieties of physical adornment and cleanliness. [To summarize]: from three *ḥadīth* concerning the *sunna* related to the body, there have arisen twelve practices. Five of them concern the head, and these are parting the hair,[23] rinsing the mouth, inhaling water to clean the nose,[24] and using the tooth stick. Three of them concern the hands and feet, and these are: trimming the nails, washing the knuckles, and cleaning the fingertips. Four of them concern the [rest of the body], and these are removing underarm hair, removing pubic hair, circumcision, and cleaning with water after urination or defecation. Narrations concerning all of these have been conveyed.

Since the purpose of this present book is to deal with outward purification, not inward, we have confined ourselves to that.

It should be kept in mind, however, that the kinds of impurities and dirt that must be removed inwardly are countless. These will be dealt with specifically in the Quarter of Perils along with how they are to be removed, and how the heart may be cleansed of them, if God most high so wills.

---

22 Abū Ṭālib al-Makkī, *Qūt al-qulūb*, 2:144, where this is attributed to al-Sarrī l-Saqaṭī.

23 Al-Bukhārī, 3558.

24 Muslim, 261.

Here ends the book, *The Mysteries of Purification* and its important aspects, which is the third book of the Quarter of Worship, from *The Revival of the Religious Sciences.*
Praise be to God [for] His help and
may blessings and salutations be
upon our beloved master and
God's Prophet Muḥammad,
and upon his
family.

This book will be followed by the
Mysteries of the Prayer.
All praise be to God alone, and may He
send blessings and salutations upon
our beloved master,
Muḥammad.

Appendix

Supplications Quoted in the *Mysteries of Purification*

1. Just before entering the toilet

بِسْمِ اللهِ أَعُوذُ بِاللهِ مِنَ الرِّجْسِ النَّجِسِ الْخَبِيثِ الْمُخْبِثِ الشَّيْطَانِ الرَّجِيم.

Bismillāh. Aʿūdhu bi-llāhi mina al-rijsi al-najisi al-khabīthi al-mukhbithi al-shayṭāni al-rajīm.

In the name of God. I take refuge in God from abomination, impurity, corruption, and the corrupter, Satan the accursed.

2. Just after leaving the toilet

الحَمْدُ لِلهِ الَّذِي أَذهَبَ عَنِّي مَا يُؤْذِينِي وأَبْقَى عَلَيَّ مَا يَنفَعُنِي

Al-ḥamdu lillāhi l-ladhī adhhaba ʿannī mā yuʾdhīnī wa-abqā ʿalayya mā yanfaʿunī.

Praise be to God who removes from me what is harmful and leaves in me what benefits me!

3. Upon completing the cleansing after urination or defecation (outside the toilet)

اللَّهُمّ طَهِّرْ قَلْبِي مِنَ النِّفاقِ وَحَصِّنْ فَرْجِي مِنَ الْفَوَاحِشِ .

Allāhumma, ṭahhir qalbī mina al-nifāq wa-ḥaṣṣin farjī mina al-fawāḥish.

O God, purify my heart from hypocrisy and guard my private parts from sin.

4. Upon beginning the ablution

بِسْمِ اللّٰهَ الرَّحْمَنِ الرَّحِيم

أَعُوذُ بِكَ مِن هَمَزَاتِ الشَّيَاطِين وَأَعُوذُ بِكَ رَبِّ أَن يَحضَرُونِ.

Bismillāh al-raḥmāni al-raḥīm.

A'ūdhu bika min hamazāti al-shayāṭīn, wa-a'ūdhu bika, Rabbi, an yaḥḍarūn.

In the name of God, the Merciful and Compassionate.
I seek refuge in You from insinuations of devils and I seek refuge in You, Lord, from their being present [with me].

5. Just before putting the hands into the vessel for ablution

اللَّهُمَّ إِنِّي أَسْأَلُكَ الْيَمْنَ وَالْبَرَكَة وَأَعُوذُ بِكَ مِنَ الشُّؤمِ وَالْهَلَكَة

Allāhumma, innī as'aluka al-yumna wa-l-baraka, wa-a'ūdhubika mina al-shu'mi wa-l-halaka.

O God, I ask of You ease and blessing and I seek refuge in You from misfortune and perdition.

6. When washing the mouth

اللَّهُمَّ أعِنِّي عَلَى تِلاَوَةِ كِتَابِك، وَكَثْرَةِ الذِّكْرِ لَك.

Allāhumma aʿinnī ʿalā tilāwati kitābika wa-kathrati al-dhikri laka.

O God, help me in the recitation of Your book and [help me] to remember You abundantly.

7. Taking water into the nose

اللَّهُمَّ أَوْجِدْنِي رَائِحَةَ الْجَنَّةِ وَأَنْتَ عَنِّي رَاض

O Allāhumma, awjidnī rāʾiḥata al-jannati wa-anta ʿannī rāḍin.

God, grant that I might smell the fragrance of heaven and that You are pleased with me.

8. Blowing water out the nose

اللَّهُمَّ إِنِّي أَعُوذُ بِكَ مِنْ رَوَائِحِ النَّارِ وَمِن سُوءِ الدَّار

Allāhumma, innī aʿūdhu bika min rāwaʾiḥi al-nār wa-min sūʾi al-dār.

O God, I seek refuge in You from the odors of the fire and the evil abode.

9. Washing the face

اللَّهُمَّ بَيِّضْ وَجْهِي بِنُورِكَ يَوْمَ تَبْيَضُّ وُجُوه أَولِيائِكَ ،

و لا تَسَوِّدْ وَجْهِي يَوْمَ تَسْوَدُّ وُجُوهُ أَعْدَائِكَ

Allāhumma, bayyiḍ wajhī bi-nūrika yawma tabyaḍḍu wujūhu awliyāʾika,

wa-lā tusawwid wajhī bi-ẓulumātika yawma taswaddu wujūhu aʿdāʾika.

O God, illuminate my face with Your light on the day when the faces of Your friends are illuminated, and do not darken my face with Your darkness on the day when the faces of Your foes are darkened.

10. Washing the right hand

اللَّهُمَّ أَعْطِنِي كِتَابِي بِيَمِينِي وَحَاسِبْنِي حِسَابًا يَسِيرًا

Allāhumma aʿṭinī kitābī bi-yamīnī wa-ḥāsibnī ḥisāban yasīran.

O God, give me my book in my right hand and reckon me with an easy reckoning.

11. Washing the left hand

اللَّهُمَّ إِني أَعُوذُبِكَ أَن تُعْطِينِي كِتَابِي بِشِمَالِيأَو مِنْ وَرَاءِ ظَهْرِي

Allāhumma innī aʿūdhu bika an tuʿṭīnī kitābī bi-shimālī aw-min warāʾi ẓahrī.

O God, I seek refuge in You from Your giving me my book in my left hand or behind my back.

12. Wiping the head

اللَّهُمَّ غَشِّنِي بِرَحْمَتِكَ ، وَأَنْزِلْ عَلَيَّ مِنْ بَرَكَاتِكَ ، وَأَظِلَّنِي تَحْتَ ظِلِّ عَرْشِكَ ، يَوْمَ لاَ ظِلَّ إلاَّ ظِلُّكَ .

Allāhumma, ghashshinī bi-raḥmatik, wa-anzil ʿalayya min barakātik, wa-aẓillanī taḥta ẓilli ʿarshika yawma lā ẓilla illā ẓilluk.

O God, cover me with Your mercy, send down upon me Your blessings, and shade me in the shade of Your throne on the day when there is no shade except Your shade.

13. Wiping the ears

اللَّهُمَّ اجْعَلْنِي مِنَ الَّذِينَ يَسْتَمِعُونَ الْقَوْلَ فَيَتَّبِعُونَ أَحْسَنَهُ ، اللَّهُمَّ أَسْمِعْنِي مُنَادِيَ الْجَنَّةِ مَعَ الأَبْرار

Allāhumma jʿalanī mina al-ladhīna yastaminʿūna al-qawla, fa-yattabiʿūna aḥsanahu, Allahumma, asmaʿī munādiya al-jannati maʿa al-abrār.

O God, make me among those who hear what is said and follow the best of it. God, let me hear the one who will call [the faithful] to heaven while I am among the righteous.

14. Wiping the back of the neck

اللّهُمَّ فَكَّ رَقَبَتِي مِنَ النَّار ، وَأَعُوذُ بِكَ مِنَ السَّلاسِلِ والأغْلاَل

Allāhumma, fakka raqabatī min al-nār, wa-aʿūdhubika mina al-salāsili wa-l-aghlāl.

O God, free me from the fire! I seek refuge in You from chains and shackles.

15. Washing the right foot

اللَّهُمَّ ثَبِّتْ قَدَمَيَّ عَلَى الصِّرَاطِ ، يَوْمَ تَزِلُّ الْأَقْدَامُ فِي النّار

Allāhumma thabbit qadamaya ʿalā al-ṣirāṭi yawma tazillu al-aqdāmu fī l-nār

O God, set my feet firmly upon the straight path on the day when feet slip into fire.

16. Washing the left foot

أَعوْذُ بِكَ أَنْ تَزِلَّ قَدَمِيَّ عَنِ الصِّرَاطِ يَوْم تَزِلُّ فِيهِ أَقدَام الْمُنَافِقِينَ

Aʿūdhu bika an tazillu qadamaya ʿani al-ṣirāti yawma tazillu al-aqdām al-munāfiqīn.

I seek refuge in You from my feet slipping on the traverse [over hell] on the day when hypocrites' feet will slip.

17. Directly after completing the ablution

أَشْهَدُ أَن لاَ إِلَهَ إِلاَّ اللهَ وَحْدَهُ لاَ شَرِيكَ لَه، وَأَشْهَدُ أَنَّ مُحَمَّداً عَبْدُهُ ورَسُولُهُ سُبْحَانَكَ اللَّهُمَّ وَبِحَمْدِكَ ، لاَ إِلَهَ إِلاَّ أَنْتَ . عَمِلْتُ سُوءاً وَظَلَمْتُ نَفسِي، أَسْتَغْفِرُكَ اللَّهُمَّ وَأَتُوبُ إِلِيكَ، فَاغْفِرْ لِي وَتُبْ عَلَيَّ، إِنَّكَ أَنْتَ التَّوَّابُ الرَّحِيمُ. اللَّهُمَّ اجْعَلْنِي مِنَ التَّوَّابِينَ وَاجْعَلْنِي مِنَ الْمُتَطَهِّرِينَ، وَاجْعَلْنِي مِن عِبَادِكَ الصَّالِحِينَ، وَاجْعَلْنِي عَبداً صَبْوراً شَكُوراً ، وَاجْعَلْنِي أَذْكُرُكَ كِثِيراً وَأُسَبِّحُكَ بُكْرَةً وَأَصِيْلاً.

Ashhadu a(n) lā ilāha illā Llāhu, waḥdahu lā sharīka lah(u), wa-ashhadu anna Muḥammadan ʿabduhu wa-rasūluhu. Subḥānak Allāhumma wa-biḥamdika, lā ilāha illā anta, ʿamiltu sūʾan wa-ẓalamtu nafsī, astaghfiruka wa-atūbu ilayk, fa-ghfir lī wa-tub ʿalaya, innaka anta al-tawwābu al-raḥīm. Allāhumma-jʿalanī mina al-tawwābīna, wa-jʿalnī mina al-mutaṭahhirīna, wa-jʿalnī min ʿibādika al-ṣāliḥīna, wa-jʿalnī ʿabdan ṣabūran shakūra, wa-jʿalnī adhkuruka dhikran kathīran, wa-usabbiḥuka bukratan wa-aṣīlā.

I bear witness that there is no god but God, alone, without partners, and I bear witness that Muḥammad is His servant and Messenger! Glory be to You, O God, and praise [be to You]! There is no god but You. I have committed evil and wronged my own soul. I seek forgiveness from You, O God, and turn to You in repentance, so forgive me and accept my repentance. You are truly the forgiving and compassionate! O God, make me among those who turn to You in repentance and make me among those who purify themselves, and make me among Your righteous servants, and make me Your patient and grateful servant, and make me someone who invokes [You] in abundance and glorifies You morning and night.

18. Upon entering the *hammām*

بِسْمِ اللهِ أَعُوذُ بِاللهِ مِنَ الرِّجْسِ النَّجِسِ الْخَبِيثِ الْمُخْبِثِ الشَّيْطَانِ الرَّجِيمِ.

Bismillāh. Aʿūdhu bi-llāhi mina al-rijsi al-najisi al-khabīthi al-mukhbithi al-shayṭāni al-rajīm.

In the name of God. I take refuge in God from abomination, impurity, corruption, and the corrupter, Satan the accursed.

Bibliography

Works in Western Languages

Harvey, L. P. *Muslims in Spain, 1500 to 1614*. Chicago: University of Chicago Press, 2005.

Keller, Nūḥ Hā Mīm. *Reliance of the Traveller: A Classic Manual of Islamic Sacred Law.* [A Translation of Aḥmad Ibn Nāqib al-Miṣrī's *Umdat al-Sālik*.] Evanston, IL: Sunna Books, 1993.

Lane-Poole, Stanley. *The Moors in Spain*. New York: G. Putnam Sons, 1903.

Lings, Martin. *What is Sufism?* Berkeley and Los Angeles: University of California Press, 1975.

Works in Arabic

Abū Dāwūd, Sulaymān b. al-Ashʿath al-Sijastānī. *Sunan*. Beirut: Dār Ibn Ḥazm, 1997.

Abū Nuʿaym al-Iṣbahānī, Aḥmad b. ʿAbdallāh. *Ḥilyat al-awliyaʾ wa-ṭabaqāt al-aṣfiyāʾ*. Beirut: Dār al-Kitāb al-ʿArabī, 1987.

al-ʿAskarī, al-Ḥassan b. ʿAbdallāh b. Saʿīd b. Ismāʿīl. *Taṣfiyāt al-Muḥaddithīn*. Cairo: al-Muṭbaʿā al-ʿArabiyya al-Ḥadītha, 1983.

al-Bayhaqī, Aḥmad b. al-Ḥusayn. *Shuʿab al-īmān*. Beirut: Dār al-Kutub al-ʿIlmiyya, 1410/1990.

———. *al-Sunan al-kubrā*. Beirut: Dār al-Maʿrifa, 1356.

al-Bazzār, Abū Bakr b. Aḥmad b. ʿAmr. *al-Baḥr al-zakhkhār* (known as *Musnad al-Bazzār*). Edited by Dr. Maḥfūẓ al-Raḥmān Zayn Allāh. Medina: Maktabat al-ʿUlūm wa-l-Ḥikam, 1988.

al-Bukhārī, Muḥammad b. Ismāʿīl b. Ibrāhīm. *al-Jāmiʿ al-ṣaḥīḥ*. Beirut: Dār Ṭawq al-Najā, 1422.

al-Dāraquṭnī, ʿAlī b. ʿUmar. *Sunan*. Beirut: Dār al-Maʿrifa, 1966.

al-Daylamī, Shīrawayh b. Shahdār. *al-Firdaws bi-maʾthūr al-khiṭṭāb = Musnad al-firdaws*. Edited by Saʿīd b. Basyūnī Zaghlūl. Beirut: Dār al-Kutub al-ʿIlmiyya, 1986.

al-Ghazālī, Abū Ḥāmid Muḥammad b. Muḥammad. *Iḥyāʾ ʿulūm al-dīn*. Jedda: Dār al-Minhāj, 2011.

Translations:

The Book of Remembrance of Death and the Afterlife. Translated by T. J. Winter. Cambridge: Islamic Texts Society, 1989.

The Mysteries of Purity. Translated by Nabih Faris. Lahore: Sh. Muhammad Ashraf, 1991.

al-Ḥākim, Abū ʿAbdallāh Muḥammad b. ʿAbdallāh. *al-Mustadrak ʿalā l-ṣaḥiḥayn*. Beirut: Dār al-Maʿrifa, 1335.

al-Haythamī, Nūr al-Dīn. *Majmaʿ al-zawāʾid wa-manbaʿ al-fawāʾid*. Beirut: Dār al-Maʿrifa, 1986.

Ibn Abī l-Dunyā, ʿAbdallāh b. Muḥammad al-Qurshī. *al-Amr bi-l-maʿrūf wa-l-nahyi ʿan al-munkar*. Beirut: Dār Ibn Ḥazm, 2004.

Ibn Abī Shayba, ʿAbdallāh b. Muḥammad. *Muṣannaf*. Edited by Muḥammad ʿAwwāma. Jedda: Dār al-Minhāj, 2006.

Ibn ʿAsākir, ʿAlī b. al-Ḥasan b. Habbat Allāh. *Tārīkh Madīna Dimashq*. Edited by Muḥibb al-Dīn ʿUmar b. Gharāma al-ʿAmrawī. Beirut: Dār al-Fikr, 1995.

Ibn Ḥanbal, Aḥmad al-Shaybānī. *Musnad*. Edited by Shuʿayb al-Arnāʿūṭ. Beirut: Muʿassasa al-Risāla, 1995.

Ibn Ḥibbān, Abū Hatim Muḥammad al-Tamimi al-Busti. *Ṣaḥīḥ*. Edited by Shuʿayb al-Arnāʿūṭ. Beirut: Muʿassasa al-Risāla, 1993.

Ibn Māja, Muḥammad b. Yazīd al-Qazwīnī. *Sunan*. Edited by Muḥammad Fuʾād ʿAbd al-Bāqī. Beirut: Dār Iḥyāʾ al-Kutub al-ʿArabiyya, 1954.

Ibn Qutayba al-Dīnawarī, ʿAbdallāh b. Muslim.*ʿUyūn al-akhbār*. Cairo: Dār al-Kutub al-Miṣriyya, 1930.

Ibn Rajab al-Ḥanbalī. *The Heirs of the Prophets*. Translated by Zaid Shakir. Chicago: Starlatch Press, 2001.

al-Makkī, Abū Ṭālib. *Qūt al-qulūb*. Edited by Muḥammad al-Zaharī al-Ghumurāwī. Cairo: al-Maṭbaʿa al-Mayymaniyya, 1310/1893. Repr. Beirut: Dār Ṣādir/Dār al-Fikr, n.d.

Mālik, Ibn Anas b. Mālik. *al-Muwaṭṭaʾ*. Edited by Muḥammad Fuʾād ʿAbd al-Bāqī. Cairo: Dār Iḥyāʾ al-Kutub al-ʿArabiyya, n.d.

al-Mundhirī, ʿAbd al-ʿAẓīm b. ʿAbd al-Qawwī. *al-Targhīb wa-l-tarhīb min al-ḥadīth al-sharīf.* Damascus: Dār Ibn Kathīr, 1999.

Muslim, Ibn al-Ḥajjāj al-Qushayrī al-Nīsābūrī. *al-Jāmiʿ al-ṣaḥīḥ*. Edited by Muḥammad Fuʾād ʿAbd al-Bāqī. Beirut: Dār Iḥyāʾ al-Kutub al-ʿArabiyya, 1954.

al-Nasāʾī, Aḥmad b. Shuʿayb. *Sunan*. Beirut: Dār al-Kitāb al-ʿArabī, 1312.

al-Nawawī, Yaḥyā b. Sharaf. *Sharḥ Ṣaḥīḥ Muslim* (known as *al-Minhāj fī sharḥ ṣaḥīḥ Muslim b. Ḥujjāj*). Damascus: Maktabat al-Ghazālī, 1349.

al-Rāfiʿī, ʿAbd al-Karīm b. Muḥammad b. ʿAbd al-Karīm. *al-Tadwīn fī akhbār Qazwīn*. Edited by ʿAzīz Allāh al-ʿAṭāridī. N.p.: Dār al-Bāz, 1987.

al-Rāzī, Fakhr al-Dīn. *al-Tafsīr al-kabīr* (known as *al-Mafātīḥ al-ghayb*). Beirut: Dār Iḥyāʾ al-Turāth al-ʿArabī, n.d.

al-Ruʿaynī, Muḥammad b. Muhammad b. ʿAbd al-Raḥmān (known as al-Ḥaṭṭāb). *Mawāhib al-jalīl li-sharḥ mukhtaṣar Khalīl*. Lebanon, Dar ʿĀlam al-Kutub, 2003.

al-Ṭabarānī, Sulaymān b. Aḥmad b. Ayyūb b. Mutayr al-Lahkmī. *al-Muʿjam al-awsāṭ*. Edited by Dr. Maḥmūd al-Ṭaḥān. N.p.: Maktaba al-Maʿārif, 1985.

———. *Muʿjam al-awsāṭ*. Cairo: Dār al-Ḥaramayn, 1995.

———. *al-Muʿjam al-ṣaghīr*. Beirut: Dār al-Kutub al-ʿIlmiyya, 1983.

———. *al-Muʿjam al-kabīr*. Edited by Ḥammadī ʿAbd al-Majīd al-Salafī. Beirut: Dār Iḥyāʾ al-Turāth al-ʿArabī, n.d.

al-Tirmidhī, al-Ḥākim. *Nawādir al-uṣūl fī maʿrifat aḥādīth al-rasūl*. Beirut: Dār al-Ṣādir, n.d.

al-Tirmidhī, Muḥammad Abū ʿĪsā b. Sawra. *al-Jāmiʿ al-ṣaḥīḥ*. Edited by Aḥmad Shākir and Muḥammad Fuʾād ʿAbd al-Bāqī. Beirut: Dār Iḥyāʾ al-Turāth al-ʿArabī, 1938.

———. *al-Shamāʾil al-Muḥammadiyya*. Beirut: Printed by Muḥammad ʿAwwāma, 2001.

al-Zabīdī, Muḥammad b. Muḥammad Murtaḍā. *Itḥāf al-sādat al-muttaqīn*. Beirut: Muʾassasat al-tārīkh al-ʿArabi, Beirut, 1994.

Index of Qurʾān Verses

Index of *Ḥadīth*

Index of Names and Places

Subject Index

ʿAbbāsid (caliphate), xiv
ablution(s), xxii–xxvi, 11, 18, 19, 29, 33–35, 38, 42, 52, 55
    dry (*tayammum*), xxii, 38–39
    greater (*ghusl*), xxii, xxiv, 37
    lesser, 23, 27–28, 32, 36–37
abomination, 24, 46, 67, 73
acts/actions, xx
Adam, sons of, 63
angel(s), xxv, 33 n.45, 50, 63
animals/creatures, 54
    cat(s), 17, 20
    dog(s), 13, 19, 20
    fish, 13
    lice, 41, 42
    mice, 17
    pig(s), 13
    worms, flies, locusts, beetles, 13
Arab(s), 43
    custom, 42
    nomadic, 52
    pagan, xxv
asceticism/ascetic(s), 59, 64
ʿ*ayniyya* (visible), 21
ayyām al-tashrīq, 37

backbiters, 57
bathhouse(s) (*ḥammām*), xxii, xxiv, xxviii, 18–19, 44–46
Bāṭinī (doctrines), xvi
beards, xxii, xxviii, 30, 36, 42, 51, 56–57, 59, 61–64
beauty, 42, 43
blame/blameworthy, xx, 60
    character (traits), 4, 5
bleach, 9
blessings, 49
blood/bleeding, 13–14, 20
    menstruation, xxv, 14, 21 n.18, 37
    post-partum, 37, 50
body, parts of. *See also* hair
    ears, 31, 35, 42, 44, 71
    eyes, 30, 54, 55
    face, 29, 35, 37, 38, 70
    feet, 6, 31, 35–37, 49, 52–53, 64
        right, 24, 31, 53, 72
        toes, 31, 53
    hand(s), 30, 35–38, 52–53, 64, 70
        right, 26, 29, 30, 38, 52–53, 70
    head, 31, 35, 36, 37, 50, 64
    mouth, 27–29, 35, 42, 51, 64, 69
    neck, 31, 71
    nose, 14, 29, 35, 64, 69
    penis, 37
    teeth, 28, 42, 44
    tongue, 42
body(ies), xxv, xxvii
bone, 14

About the Translators

Mohamed Fouad Aresmouk

After growing up in a traditional Marrakesh family, the son of an Arabic teacher and grandson of one of the most renowned Qurʾān teachers in Marrakesh, Fouad Aresmouk completed his degree in Islamic Studies and Arabic at Qadi Ayyad University, Marrakesh. He is the author of *al-Rashād fī zabdat al-awrād*, a mystical commentary on the litany of the Habibiyya Sufi order of Morocco; this work is presently being prepared for publication.

Michael Abdurrahman Fitzgerald

Originally from California, Abdurrahman Fitzgerald and his wife migrated to Morocco in the late 1970s. Since that time, he has been involved in education and the study of Arabic, Islam, and Sufism for the past thirty years. He co-translated *Ibn al-Qayyim on the Invocation of God* (Islamic Text Society, 2000), worked on the editing and annotation of Denys Johnson-Davies's translation of al-Ghāzali's *Kitāb ādab al-akl* (Islamic Texts Society, 2000), and also on Dr. Kenneth Honerkamp's edition of *al-Rasāʾil al-kubrā* by Ibn ʿAbbād (Dār al-Machreq, 2005). Other works translated with Fouad Aresmouk include *The Immense Ocean*, a portion of Ibn ʿAjība's Qurʾānic commentary; *The Book of Ascension*, Ibn ʿAjība's spiritual glossary; and a portion of the work, *Two Sufi Commentaries*, all published by Fons Vitae. Abdurrahman holds degrees from the University of California and Shenandoah University, Virginia, and is the director of the Center for Language and Culture, Marrakesh.

This publication was made possible through the generosity of international donors and through the support of a grant from the John Templeton Foundation. The opinions expressed in this publication are those of its authors and do not necessarily reflect the views of the John Templeton Foundation.